FAST FORWARD

*ACCELERATE YOUR SPIRITUAL
LIFE THROUGH FASTING*

All Scripture quotations, unless otherwise indicated, are taken from the New King James Version®. Copyright © 1982 by Thomas Nelson. Used by permission. All rights reserved.

Scripture quotations marked (NIV) are taken from the Holy Bible, New International Version®, NIV®. Copyright © 1973, 1978, 1984, 2011 by Biblica, Inc.™ Used by permission of Zondervan. All rights reserved worldwide. www.zondervan.com The "NIV" and "New International Version" are trademarks registered in the United States Patent and Trademark Office by Biblica, Inc.™

Scripture quotations marked (ESV) are from the ESV® Bible (The Holy Bible, English Standard Version®), Copyright © 2001 by Crossway, a publishing ministry of Good News Publishers. Used by permission. All rights reserved. May not copy or download more than 500 consecutive verses of the ESV Bible or more than one half of any book of the ESV Bible.

Scripture quotations marked (NLT) are taken from the Holy Bible, New Living Translation copyright © 1996, 2004, 2007, 2013, 2015 by Tyndale House Foundation. Used by permission of Tyndale House Publishers Inc., Carol Stream, Illinois 60188. All rights reserved.

ISBN: 978-1-951201-11-1

CONTENTS

Introduction: Fast Forward — v
ABC's of Fasting — ix

1. Power is not in Fasting — 1
2. Go Far to Find Fire — 7
3. Spirit-Led Fast — 15
4. Fasting is More Challenging Mentally Than Physically — 21
5. Comfort Eating — 29
6. Flying First Class — 37
7. Bowl for Blessing — 45
8. Fasting is Feasting — 51
9. Weight, Not Worth — 59
10. The Way of Humility — 65
11. From Crisis to Calling — 73
12. Threefold Cord — 81
13. Building, Binding, and Birthing — 91
14. Fast to Get First Love — 99
15. Private Discipline, Public Reward — 107
16. Go Deeper — 115
17. Gold, Silver, and Precious Stones — 123
18. Viral Revival — 131
19. Be a Finisher, Not a Quitter — 139
20. Someone is Living in Revival — 145
21. From Grapes to Glory — 153

Appendix 1: About the Author — 161
Appendix 2: Other Books — 162
Appendix 3: Online School — 163
Appendix 4: Stay Connected — 164
Appendix 5: References — 165
Appendix 6: Credits — 166

INTRODUCTION: FAST FORWARD

> But you, when you fast, anoint your head and wash your face.
>
> Matthew 6:17

Our human body was designed by God to be able to fast. Did you know that when you sleep, you are fasting? That's why the first meal of the day is called breakfast—it's when you break your fast. Scientific research tells us that a lot of repairing takes place in our bodies when we fast. So, good news, you've been already sort of secretly fasting all your life.

Hence, I'm inviting you to go to another level, beyond just the 8 hours of not eating because you are sleeping. Fasting accelerates your spiritual life. I want to make it clear that fasting is not starvation, a diet, or a hunger strike. It's not treatment for weight loss either. Biblical fasting is going without food for the purpose of seeking God. Diets focus on losing weight, fasting is focused on God. By the way, biblical fasting is not turning off your social media or abstaining from coffee or sweets, although, such steps will help you during a fast. Fasting according to the Bible is going without food for the purpose of seeking God.

FAST FORWARD

Yes, it's NO food for spiritual reasons.

I know you're thinking, Vlad, you're crazy. Who in their right mind would willingly do that? Well, actually many noteworthy people mentioned in the Bible practiced fasting: Moses, David, Elijah, Esther, Daniel, Anna, and Paul, just to name a few. Even our Lord Jesus practiced fasting; in fact, He didn't start His ministry without it. When Jesus taught His disciples about fasting, He said, *"when you fast"*, not *"if you fast"* (Matthew 6:16). He assumed that we would willingly fast as a part of our normal lives.

Fasting is not fun for the flesh, that's for sure. Yet, fasting is an incredibly powerful weapon used to bring spiritual acceleration into your life. I don't know of any other discipline that gives the flesh a black eye as much as fasting does. Many Christians have their spiritual life hijacked by their flesh and soul. I was like that too. Truth is, the more we feed our lower nature which Jesus defeated, the more we create hinderances in our spiritual progress. Fasting unhinders our spiritual life. It creates a domino effect on the rest of the disciplines in our life.

Fasting helps to get the fire going, but it's also fuel for more fire. If you want to go further in Christ, you must do what Christ taught us to do – "when you fast". I encourage you to make fasting a habit.

Let me remind you of one promise that makes the process of fasting more endurable. Jesus said, *"When you fast, anoint your head and wash your face, so that you do not appear to men to be fasting, but to your Father who is in the secret place; and your Father who sees in secret will reward you openly"* (Matthew 6:17).

FAST FORWARD: INTRODUCTION

That is right! When you fast biblically, the Father rewards you openly. Jesus motivates us toward this spiritual discipline with reward. When our motive is to attract the attention of our Father or to the Spirit's prompting, there is a reward. Let this truth sink in.

God will reward you for fasting. Let that sink in. When fasting, it's important to replace eating with reading God's word. But God will reward you even if you don't read more of the Scriptures than you usually do. God will reward you even if you don't pray more than you usually pray. Fasting will lead you to deeper prayer and greater hunger for God's word; however, God promises us a reward for simply fasting. I used to think that God rewards us in fasting by refining us spiritually. There is some truth in that, simply because most of the work God does during our fast is inside of us. However, Jesus Himself stated that the Heavenly Father will reward us openly, not just in secret.

That's why I titled this book Fast Forward. I believe that fasting creates a forward motion in your life toward God's plans and purposes. Fasting would not require you to do more but actually to do less (eating). It brings spiritual acceleration into your walk with God.

So, don't get scared to start fasting. The promise of God to reward you is waiting to be fulfilled in your life. The process of God reviving you is waiting to be kickstarted in your life. When you begin fasting, make up your mind to stick with it.

I will immediately advise you to speak with your healthcare provider before you begin any type of fasting. I am not a doctor nor a medical professional. Therefore, this book is not a medical publication. Use wisdom. If you have a medical condition you should consult with your doctor. Each person must be led by the Lord. I am not pushing you to take a 21-day fast, I'm encouraging you to start a biblical discipline of fasting.

Now, when it comes to how many days you should fast and what type of fast you should do as well as how to prepare for it, please read next section: *ABC's of fasting*.

THE ABC'S OF FASTING

What is Fasting?

Biblical fasting is not starvation or an involuntary absence of food; it is abstaining from food for spiritual reasons. Fasting is not a hunger strike, and it is not a diet—a diet focuses on helping you lose weight, it is a spiritual discipline that draws you closer to God. Fasting helps to find fulfillment in God's calling on your life, as well as subdue your flesh with all its conflicts. You can fast for different reasons, such as to overcome problems and challenges or to restore your hunger and passion for God.

Types of Fasts

There are different types of fasts. There is an **absolute fast,** going without food or water, sometimes referred to as a dry fast. Moses went on this type of fast for 40 days; and it was supernatural (Exodus 34:28). The city of Nineveh fasted like this for three days (Jonah 3:7) as well as the apostle Paul after his encounter with the Lord (Acts 9:9). Caution: This should NOT be undertaken for more than three days, and it should only be done if you have a clear directive from the Lord and are in good health. Another fast is called a **normal fast** or a full fast. This is when you don't eat and only drink water. We believe that Jesus went on this type of fast for 40 days. The Bible says He ate nothing, but it doesn't mention that He didn't drink anything: "*...Being tempted for forty days by the devil. And in those days He ate nothing, and afterward, when they had ended, He was hungry*" (Luke 4:2). Usually, if a person in the Bible didn't drink anything during their fast Scripture would point that out.

A **partial fast**, commonly referred to as a Daniel Fast, is where you abstain from certain foods. This fast usually includes eating no meat, no sweets, no dairy or other pleasant foods—only soups, fruits, and vegetables. This fast is named after the prophet Daniel: "*I ate no pleasant food, no meat or wine came into my mouth, nor did I anoint myself at all, till three whole weeks were fulfilled*" (Daniel 10:3). For me, this is the hardest fast. I don't think I have ever done more than seven days because I don't like fasting and thinking about food at the same time. Plus, eating an entire meal and still feeling hungry is a tougher challenge for me than simply not eating at all.

The last type of fast is a **corporate fast**. Your private fasting should be done in secret as Jesus instructed in Matthew 6:16, but there is also a public fast which is proclaimed by leaders. There are a few biblical examples of this, such as the prophet Samuel calling an entire nation to a fast (1 Samuel 7:6); Esther calling her Jewish people to a fast (Esther 4:16); Ezra proclaiming a fast (Ezra 8:21–23); the pagan king of Nineveh declaring a fast to his nation (Jonah 3:5); and the disciples fasting and ministering to the Lord (Acts 13:2–3).

As a reminder, we are to examine our hearts so that we practice periods of fasting to be noticed by the Lord, not by the eyes of man.

How to Fast

Set a goal

No matter what type of fast you begin, you must have a reason and a goal! Be specific. Why are you fasting? Do you want to get closer to God and be more sensitive to the spiritual realm? Do you need direction in life's decisions, healing, restoration of your marriage, help with family issues, or wisdom? Are you facing financial difficulties? Ask the Holy Spirit for guidance. Decide what to fast for and present it constantly to God in prayer.

Decide on the type of fast

The type of fast you choose is between you and the Lord. You could go on a full fast in which you only drink liquids. You may desire to fast like Daniel, who abstained from sweets and meats, and the only liquid he drank was water. Pay attention to what the Holy Spirit leads you to do and do it.

FAST FORWARD

Choose length

Also, decide how long you will fast. Remember that you may fast as long as you like, as the Lord leads. Be courteous enough to inform those who prepare meals for you or share meals with you about your plans to fast. Most people can easily fast from 1 to 3 days, but you may feel God's grace to go longer, even 21 to 40 days. Use wisdom and pray for guidance. Beginners are advised to start slowly.

Plan ahead

Choose days that fit your schedule, take into consideration that you might feel extra tired. When you fast, your body eliminates toxins from your system. This can cause mild discomfort, such as headaches and irritability during withdrawal from caffeine and sugars. And naturally, you will have hunger pains. Hunger is a common side effect of any fast. Avoiding water can make you feel even hungrier, since water helps increase satiety. If you don't eat food or drink water, your body begins to crave fuel. You will likely feel fatigued, dizzy, and weak. David said of his fasting, *"My knees are weak through fasting, and my flesh is feeble from lack of fatness"* (Psalm 109:24).

One of the other things we often feel during a fast is irritability. As the hunger builds up, you're bound to feel cranky. Mood swings are pretty common. Also, when you're tired and hungry, it can be difficult to concentrate at school or work. So limit your activity, use good common sense, and exercise moderately. Take time to rest.

Set aside time each day

Quiet yourself before the Lord, meditate on His Word, and write down what He would be saying to you. Fasting brings about miraculous results. You are following Jesus's example when you fast. Spend time listening to praise and worship music. Constantly read and meditate on the Word. Let the hunger pangs remind you to stop everything and pray—and pray as often as you can throughout the day. Get away from normal distractions as much as possible, and keep your heart and mind set on seeking the face of God.

End the fast slowly

Of course, how much time you need to resume your regular diet depends on what you fast from and for how long. If it was only a one-day fast, then usually there is no harm to resume normal eating. If you go for more than three days, you must begin eating solid food very gradually; eat small portions or snacks. When the time comes to end your fast, eating solid foods too soon and/or overeating can be extremely dangerous to your digestive system.

DAY ONE

POWER IS NOT IN FASTING

> Once God has spoken; twice have I heard this: that power belongs to God, and that to you, O Lord, belongs steadfast love. For you will render to a man according to his work.
>
> Psalm 62:11–12 ESV

The first time I fasted was when I had just arrived in the United States as an immigrant refugee from the Ukraine. My parents were involved in a church plant that got started in someone's living room. They would fast every Wednesday and meet in the evening at that location, praying for God to bless the new church, known today as Hungry Generation Church. Even as a fourteen-year-old, I was moved by the vision of my pastor and decided to join the adults fasting every Wednesday.

This practice of fasting 24 hours once a week continued for many years, and over those years I saw the Lord fill me more and more with the Holy Spirit. When I battled with an addiction to pornography, fasting helped to put my flesh under control and prepare me for the deliverance I desperately needed. When I became a youth pastor at the age of sixteen, I continued to fast every Wednesday and dedicate that day to the Lord, spending time in the Word and prayer. In fact, I even missed school every week on that day to spend time with God. (I was doing fine in school and would catch up with all class assignments later during the week). On one of those Wednesdays, the Lord touched me powerfully and called me into full-time ministry.

Later in life, I had a difficult time getting married. There was some sort of mental stronghold or curse in my mind—I couldn't make decisions and I would always second-guess myself. On my first date with Lana, the woman who would become my wife, I expressed my indecisive feelings, and then I broke up with her the next day. My mind was a mess! A few weeks after that break-up, our church went on a 21-day fast in the month of January, and I joined that fast. God broke something off of my mind. To make a long story short, all my indecisiveness was broken; I reconnected with Lana, and eight months later we were married. It has now been over 11 years since we were married, and I am a very blessed man! I am so glad that I joined the group in fasting that year.

Let me make this clear: Even though fasting brings you closer to breakthrough and has many benefits, it doesn't have any power in and of itself, nor does it produce power. All the power is in God. Power might flow through fasting, but it does not come from fasting. Fasting doesn't move God; it moves us closer to Him.

POWER IS NOT IN FASTING

If you turn on the faucet and water starts running, nothing will come into your cup unless you move your cup directly under the faucet. That's what fasting does—it moves us to be under the flow of God's grace and power. Faith turns on the faucet and fasting moves the flesh out of the way so that our spirit can be sensitive to the Holy Spirit.

FAST FORWARD

⭕ *Prayer*

God, I choose to surrender my fleshly desires in order to come closer to You. Help me to shift my focus from my needs to Your will for my life.

What is your reason for beginning this fast? What is your goal?

POWER IS NOT IN FASTING

Scriptures to meditate on:

1. After these things I heard a loud voice of a great multitude in heaven, saying, "Alleluia! Salvation and glory and honor and power *belong* to the Lord our God…" And I heard, as it were, the voice of a great multitude, as the sound of many waters and as the sound of mighty thunderings, saying, "Alleluia! For the Lord God Omnipotent reigns!"

Revelation 19:1, 6

2. And do not lead us into temptation, but deliver us from the evil one. For Yours is the kingdom and the power and the glory forever. Amen.

Matthew 6:13

3. For the kingdom is the Lord's, and He rules over the nations.

Psalm 22:28

FASTING TIP

Our body is accustomed to consuming food at regular intervals during the day. As you refrain from eating, it is normal to experience dizziness, weakness, headaches, nausea, etc. These symptoms can be common during any long-term fast.

DAY TWO

GO FAR
TO FIND FIRE

> One day Moses was tending the flock of his father-in-law, Jethro, the priest of Midian. He led the flock far into the wilderness and came to Sinai, the mountain of God.
>
> Exodus 3:1 NLT

In December of 2020, the Lord prompted me to lead our church in a 21-day fast starting the following month. I was a bit terrified because I personally had never actually finished an entire 21-day fast. The last time I had tried was 11 years earlier when I had those decision-making issues. I stopped the fast on the 17th day because I was too weak and had started to faint. I was also unable to sleep for a few nights in a row. Frightened by this, I stopped the fast early. All those years, I had not attempted another 21-day fast. Instead, I simply continued to be faithful with a three-day period of fasting each month. That was doable.

However, I sensed a prompting to start again because I felt that something was about to change in my life and my ministry. But in my mind, there was an electric fence around what I was comfortable with. I was afraid to go farther because I thought I would die. That negative physical experience 11 years before created this belief in my mind that prolonged fasting was dangerous and would kill me. I knew the Lord was calling me to climb over the fence of my fears and get outside of the comfort zone of what was familiar and safe.

The story of Moses came to my mind. While enjoying the glory and comforts of Egypt, Moses was moved by the suffering of his people. He attempted to deliver Israel by his own strength and killed an Egyptian, which resulted in him being on Pharaoh's "most wanted" list. Instead of liberating Israel, he got into trouble. He got burned trying to do the work of God in his own power, so he ran for his life. He got married, got a job, had kids, and settled down to a quiet normal life.

But something was missing. He was born to be more than that. God didn't rescue him from crocodiles as an infant to only live and work in a desert. God did not allow him to be trained in the palace to spend his life wandering around with sheep. Maybe you are like Moses, burned out by your service to God. You know you have a greater destiny, but you feel stuck in life. Perhaps you are tired of going around the same mountain. You know you have a purpose, but you are wasting your life living in passivity!

Everything changed for Moses when he did something different. On one of those ordinary days, Moses decided to go "far into the wilderness." This was outside of his routine, beyond the radius of what was usual to him. He went far beyond what was familiar and there he met fire—a burning bush, and Moses encountered the Lord there. Moses's insecurities were exposed, his calling was revealed, and the power of God was released into his life. He would never be the same.

That burning bush became the turning point for Moses and for Israel. The disappointment of failing to deliver Israel by his political strength was turned into divine appointment, which empowered him to go with the power of God to deliver the enslaved nation.

God's solution for burned-out believers is a "burning bush". The burning bush sets burned-out souls on fire for God. There is just one thing: the burning bush is found outside of what is routine, familiar, normal, and predictable. Only there will you find the all-consuming fire of the Holy Spirit that will move you forward.

You must climb over the fence of your fears. Get out of your rut and routine. Go further than normal. You will be surprised at what is waiting for you there. You will find an encounter, a fire, a burning bush, a call of God, and empowerment. That's what happened to Moses, and that is what is going to happen to you!

Go far to find new fire.

FAST FORWARD

> ○ *Prayer*

Heavenly Father, thank You for Your call on my life. Help me to surrender to You every fear and limitation that prevents me from walking closer with You. I am making a decision today to seek You. I surrender, and I will allow You to take me where I'm not comfortable going, in order to know You and to bring others to You to be saved.

 Ponder

What limitations do you feel God wants to break in your life or mind during this fast?

GO FAR TO FIND FIRE

Scriptures to meditate on:

For the Lord your God is a consuming fire, a jealous God.

Deuteronomy 4:24

For our God is a consuming fire.

Hebrews 12:29

John answered, saying to all, "I indeed baptize you with water; but One mightier than I is coming, whose sandal strap I am not worthy to loose. He will baptize you with the Holy Spirit and fire.

Luke 3:16

Who makes His angels spirits, His ministers a flame of fire.

Psalm 104:4

Not lagging in diligence, fervent in spirit, serving the Lord.

Romans 12:11

FAST FORWARD

6 And the fire on the altar shall be kept burning on it; it shall not be put out. And the priest shall burn wood on it every morning, and lay the burnt offering in order on it; and he shall burn on it the fat of the peace offerings.

Leviticus 6:12

7 I know your works, that you are neither cold nor hot. I could wish you were cold or hot. So then, because you are lukewarm, and neither cold nor hot, I will vomit you out of My mouth. Because you say, 'I am rich, have become wealthy, and have need of nothing'—and do not know that you are wretched, miserable, poor, blind, and naked— I counsel you to buy from Me gold refined in the fire, that you may be rich; and white garments, that you may be clothed, that the shame of your nakedness may not be revealed; and anoint your eyes with eye salve, that you may see. As many as I love, I rebuke and chasten. Therefore be zealous and repent. Behold, I stand at the door and knock. If anyone hears My voice and opens the door, I will come in to him and dine with him, and he with Me.

Revelation 3:15–20

FASTING TIP

"This stage is when your body transitions into fasting mode and, for many people, it's the most challenging part of their fast. This stage is where you start to feel the hunger pangs as you skip your regular mealtime routine." [1]

DAY THREE

SPIRIT-LED FAST

> When You said, "Seek My face," my heart said to You, "Your face, LORD, I will seek."
>
> Psalm 27:8

On the sixth day of the 21-day fast we had begun as a church, I was in California speaking at a morning session for my friend David Diga Hernandez. Pastor Benny Hinn preached the evening service, and during the time of worship, I felt a strong touch of God prompting me to expand my 21-day fast to a 40-day fast. My immediate thought was that it was only the 6th day—I had yet to get to 21, and now I was getting these strong thoughts and impressions to make up my mind to go for 40.

The Spirit impressed a scripture on my heart about Jesus starting His ministry with a 40-day fast. After that fast, *"the devil left Him, and behold, angels came and ministered to Him"* (Matthew 4:11), and *"Jesus returned in the power of the Spirit to Galilee, and news of Him went out through all the surrounding region"* (Luke 4:14). It was one of those times when I knew that I knew that I knew the Holy Spirit was calling me to go "far into the wilderness" and follow the example of the Lord. If Jesus didn't start His ministry without a fast, then who am I to advance my full-time ministry without an extended period of fasting? If after those 40 days of fasting Jesus returned with power, we have a promise from His example that after an extended period of fasting some devils will leave, angels will come, and we will return in power.

"Demons will leave" meant for me that some things in the ministry that shouldn't be there would be broken. "Angels will come" meant that divine connections would occur. "Returning in power" meant that there would be a greater measure of God's power in the ministry.

I was on my knees when this download took place. I got up, with tears rolling down my cheeks, and I told my wife with a very serious face, "I am going for 40." She also sensed that something had just happened to me.

We don't have to be led by the Holy Spirit to fast. Fasting is just a part of being a disciple of Jesus Christ. Following Jesus and being His disciple means living a life of self-denial—and fasting helps with that. That being said, you can choose how and when to fast, but it's completely different when God Himself chooses a fast for you, as the prophet Isaiah said: *"Is it a fast that I have chosen... an acceptable day to the Lord?"* (Isaiah 58:5). When God invites you to a fast, obey Him. The Holy Spirit led Jesus into a prolonged fast and He led Him into the wilderness (Matthew 4:1).

SPIRIT-LED FAST

When the Holy Spirit leads you to fast, He supplies you with His strength for that fast, no matter how long it is.

FAST FORWARD

○ *Prayer*

Holy Spirit, as I dedicate these days to You in fasting and prayer, I ask that You break off every limitation in my mind. Take me as deep and as far as You want. Help me to not limit You or what You desire to do in me. Strengthen me as I learn to follow You through this fast.

Ponder

What do you feel the Holy Spirit is saying to you today?

SPIRIT-LED FAST

Scriptures to meditate on:

1 When You said, "Seek My face," my heart said to You, "Your face, Lord, I will seek."

Psalm 27:8

2 Draw me away! We will run after you. The king has brought me into his chambers. We will be glad and rejoice in you. We will remember your love more than wine. Rightly do they love you.

Song of Solomon 1:4

3 Then Jesus was led up by the Spirit into the wilderness to be tempted by the devil.

Matthew 4:1

4 Is it a fast that I have chosen, a day for a man to afflict his soul? Is it to bow down his head like a bulrush, and to spread out sackcloth and ashes? Would you call this a fast, and an acceptable day to the Lord?

Isaiah 58:5

FASTING TIP

If you feel occasional hunger, drink a glass of water and rest. You should also replace your usual mealtimes with Scripture reading to help your spirit overcome your flesh in moments of weakness.

DAY FOUR

FASTING IS MORE CHALLENGING MENTALLY THAN PHYSICALLY

> "Do not fear, Daniel, for from the first day that you set your heart to understand, and to humble yourself before your God, your words were heard; and I have come because of your words."
>
> Daniel 10:12

In the middle of my 40-day fast, I took a trip to Ukraine to preach at a church. The only reason I agreed to do this was because my pastor said that I should. He had done a 40-day fast before and I trusted his wisdom in this. Someone blessed us with first-class tickets to Ukraine. It was my first time flying first class on an international flight—a totally different experience from normal flying. I had a bed, pillow, and blankets. A flight attendant asked what we wanted to order for dinner. Now, my wife wasn't fasting. While I was fasting, she was feasting — so she requested a delicious meal. She was sitting right next to me. Man, that meal looked so good! I wasn't hungry, but it was torture knowing that food was available.

FAST FORWARD

It was my first time going to Ukraine in 20 years, and I was flying first class. Thoughts started going through my head: Just stop the fast for three days. Enjoy your life and then resume the fast after the trip. I knew it was from the devil, because if I ate the meal they offered as my first meal after 20 days of fasting, I would get instantly sick and could potentially hurt my stomach and die. Also, I was already halfway through the fast.

I learned something very quickly that day: fasting is more difficult mentally than physically. In fact, fasting exposes how weak we are mentally. The first few days of fasting are usually uncomfortable physically with headaches, fatigue, mood swings, etc., but after that it's smooth sailing.

I couldn't understand one verse about fasting until I experienced it myself: *"And when He had fasted forty days and forty nights, afterward He was hungry"* (Matthew 4:2). It says Jesus was hungry after 40 days of fasting. I used to read this and think there must be a mistake, because I get hungry after 40 minutes of fasting. Well, maybe it was because Jesus was so sinless that He didn't get hungry for something that we mortals get tempted with. But then again, we know that Jesus was 100% God and 100% human. Jesus had the same physical needs that we have. He got hungry after 40 days. I experienced the same thing after my 40-day commitment to fasting. No, I am not like Jesus—not even close yet.

It is interesting that when Jesus felt hungry is when Satan tempted Him with food. That was the first temptation of the Lord in the wilderness. I truly believe that is what happens during fasting. The enemy will play mind games to make people stop fasting, even if they are not hungry physically. Most of the temptation during fasting happens in our head, not in our belly, in other words they are mental, not physical. That doesn't mean there is no physical hardship when you fast, but my point is that most of the time fasting is more challenging to your mind than to your stomach.

In fact, we see that with Daniel. God saw Daniel when he set his heart to humble himself, which in the original Hebrew is another word for fasting. From the first day that he set his heart to fast, God had already answered his petitions.

I want to share a secret with you of how to finish your fast. Make up your mind to complete your fast before you even begin. Every time I start a fast with the mentality of, "I will see how I feel," I never finish it. Thoughts like that are an open door for temptation to lure you out of what God has called you to do. Once you make up your mind to fast, you will realize how powerful thoughts are. God responds to them. You will be able to overcome your mental temptations to eat if you have already made up your mind to fulfill your commitment.

If an emergency should arise that causes you to stop, don't feel guilty if you can't finish your fast. However, making up your mind first adds determination to your decision to go through with it. Once you complete the fast, your mind gets clearer, and your willpower gets stronger. The devil will try to mess with your head during a fast—resist him with the Word.

FAST FORWARD

Make up your mind! Stick with your decision to fast. Add determination to that decision to finish your fast. If it's worth starting, it's worth finishing!

FASTING IS MORE CHALLENGING MENANTALLY THAN PHYSICALLY

O Prayer

God, thank You for the desire You birthed in me to fast. I pray that You would help me to remain strong in my decision to die to myself through this act of fasting. Holy Spirit, I pray for Your grace, supernatural strength, and clarity in my mind.

✸ Ponder

As you fast today, what are you experiencing physically, mentally, emotionally, and spiritually? Write it down.

FAST FORWARD

Scriptures to meditate on:

1 Then he said to me, "Do not fear, Daniel, for from the first day that you set your heart to understand, and to humble yourself before your God, your words were heard; and I have come because of your words.

Daniel 10:12

2 If then you were raised with Christ, seek those things which are above, where Christ is, sitting at the right hand of God. Set your mind on things above, not on things on the earth.

Colossians 3:1–2

3 Finally, brethren, whatever things are true, whatever things are noble, whatever things are just, whatever things are pure, whatever things are lovely, whatever things are of good report, if there is any virtue and if there is anything praiseworthy—meditate on these things… I can do all things through Christ who strengthens me.

Philippians 4:8, 13

FASTING IS MORE CHALLENGING MENANTALLY THAN PHYSICALLY

I beseech you therefore, brethren, by the mercies of God, that you present your bodies a living sacrifice, holy, acceptable to God, which is your reasonable service. And do not be conformed to this world, but be transformed by the renewing of your mind, that you may prove what is that good and acceptable and perfect will of God.

Romans 12:1–2

Keep your heart with all diligence, for out of it spring the issues of life.

Proverbs 4:23

FASTING TIP

Typically, about day 3–5 on a fast the body understands that there is no food intake and begins to shut down the production of digestive juices in order to conserve energy. At this point, you may no longer experience hunger for some days.

DAY FIVE

COMFORT EATING

> It is a sabbath of solemn rest for you, and you shall afflict your souls. It is a statute forever.
>
> Leviticus 16:31

Fasting exposes the unhealthy relationship we have with food. Good food makes people feel happy, so they often quench their negative emotions or boredom with eating. When you fast, you are forced to deal with those toxic emotions in a new way, by bringing them to the Holy Spirit instead of finding false comfort in food. Fasting trains us to share our feelings with the Father, instead of with the fridge or the pantry.

Food is a gift from God. Paul said so in 1 Timothy: "For every creature of God is good, and nothing is to be refused if it is received with thanksgiving" (1 Timothy 4:4). But food was never given to fix our emotional problems. God never intended food to be your friend! He created food to fuel your body for the purpose of living. It's like gasoline—you don't fall in love with fuel and gas stations, although they are necessary to run your car. It is the same with food. We must be in love with God, not nourishment. We can derive pleasure and satisfaction from delicious food, but we should remember that its main purpose is to nourish our body. When we use food as a source of emotional pleasure or as a way of dealing with stress and anxiety, we make it an idol.

When you comfort yourself with food, you can also fall into the sin of gluttony. Gluttony is an ongoing act of overeating and drinking. It abuses God's natural order for hunger, which is intended to cause you to seek necessary nourishment for your body. Ezekiel says that Sodom had this issue: they were *"arrogant, overfed, and unconcerned"* (Ezekiel 16:49 NIV). Solomon says that *"the drunkard and the glutton will come to poverty"* (Proverbs 23:21). So not only is gluttony a sin of idolatry, and brings poverty, but it also has the potential of bringing a person to obesity, which can result in many physical ailments.

Israel was commanded to fast once a year on the Day of Atonement. The command for this fast was, *"you shall afflict your souls"* (Leviticus 16:31). Fasting is an affliction of the soul. I find it interesting that it doesn't say it afflicts your body, as fasting seems like a physical affliction. But here we see fasting as a suffering of the soul (the seat of your mind, will, and emotions). So fasting afflicts, humbles, and weakens your soul's control. We don't need to fast for our spirit, since it's already sealed by the Holy Spirit and made perfect by Jesus's sacrifice. Our spirit is not the problem; our soul is.

COMFORT EATING

Fasting helps to move us from being soulish Christians to being spiritual Christians by putting the soul where it belongs: in the back seat. Many believers let their souls control their lives instead of their spirits, but fasting helps to break dominion of your soul over you. That is why when you fast, your soul will throw a fit; you might feel cranky and irritable, useless, doubtful, mentally attacked, or second guess yourself, but that's totally normal—it's an affliction of the soul. Pray hard. Don't give up.

During your fast, not only will physical toxins be removed, but emotional toxins will as well. Allow the Holy Spirit to cleanse you of soul toxins during the fast.

FAST FORWARD

○ *Prayer*

God, thank You for this time in which You are exposing things within my heart. Forgive me for any sin of gluttony or overdrinking that I have used to numb my emotions. Forgive me for making food an idol by wanting it to comfort me, instead of coming to You. I want to stop running to other sources for relief. I surrender to You. Holy Spirit, help me to find comfort in You alone.

❄ *Ponder*

What is the Holy Spirit guiding you to do or surrender today?

COMFORT EATING

Scriptures to meditate on:

1. For every creature of God is good, and nothing is to be refused if it is received with thanksgiving.

1 Timothy 4:4

2. But food does not commend us to God; for neither if we eat are we the better, nor if we do not eat are we the worse.

1 Corinthians 8:8

3. Whose end is destruction, whose god is their belly, and whose glory is in their shame—who set their mind on earthly things.

Philippians 3:19

4. Look, this was the iniquity of your sister Sodom: She and her daughter had pride, fullness of food, and abundance of idleness; neither did she strengthen the hand of the poor and needy.

Ezekiel 16:49

FAST FORWARD

Do not mix with winebibbers, or with gluttonous eaters of meat; For the drunkard and the glutton will come to poverty, and drowsiness will clothe a man with rags.

Proverbs 23:20-21

It is a sabbath of solemn rest for you, and you shall afflict your souls. It is a statute forever.

Leviticus 16:31

FASTING TIP

Bowel movements and bad breath are two subjects that most people usually avoid discussing, but when fasting, you need to be aware of both. Bad breath will be a concern throughout every stage of a fast. Slightly offensive breath is completely natural and part of the detoxing process. [1]

DAY SIX

FLYING FIRST CLASS

> Then Jesus said to His disciples, "If anyone desires to come after Me, let him deny himself, and take up his cross, and follow Me."
>
> Matthew 16:24

Preaching in other places has made me depend a lot on flying. I love flying way more than driving. It's much faster, and I don't have to be stuck behind the wheel. I have learned many truths about the Lord and life in general from my flying experiences. For example, one time we missed our flight to Germany in Denver because we were in the airport drinking coffee and lost track of time. We ran to our gate only to see the plane moving slowly away onto the tarmac. We felt like we were in the movie Left Behind or among the five foolish virgins. That's how people are with God—they come to church (the airport) but miss Christ (the plane) who can take them to heaven.

Recently, I had another revelation. As I mentioned, I was flying first class overseas during my extended fast. I had never flown first class before. It was all so new to me. The seats were different, the food was different, the service was different... honestly, a totally different experience. This is crazy though—I was in the same airplane with the same pilot, but I had a completely different experience. What made the difference between my first-class seat and seat 57 by the bathroom? The price! Those in the first-class section of the plane paid much more to have that seat than those in the economy class.

Could it be the same with Christianity? Every Christian is in Christ, but not every Christian has the same experience with Him. Some Christians are full of the world; others are full of the Word. Some Christians live trying to discover themselves, while others live to discover God; some are embracing themselves and enjoying life, others are denying themselves. Some live very shallow lives, while others live supernatural ones. It is all about the price you are willing to pay.

But remember, we don't earn our salvation by living a surrendered life.

Jesus calls those who were far from Him to believe in Him, and those who believe in Him to follow Him. Believing in Jesus gets you onto the plane, but closely following Him puts you in a first-class seat, nearer to Him, the Pilot. Believing in Jesus is the starting gate that gets us to heaven, but then we must grow to become His disciples.

FLYING FIRST CLASS

A believer *comes to the cross*	A disciple *gets on the cross*
A believer *retreats to safety*	A disciple *embraces suffering*
A believer *comes to church*	A disciple *is the church*
A believer *cheers from the sidelines*	A disciple *is in the game*
A believer *reads the Word*	A disciple *lives it*
A believer *is all about believing in Jesus*	A disciple *is all about being like Jesus*
A believer *is comfort-driven*	A disciple *is purpose-driven, making sacrifices*
A believer *talks*	A disciple *raises disciples and leads by example*

FAST FORWARD

Disciples establish discipline. One mark that separates disciples from believers is their self-denial. It is a decision to die to oneself, pick up their cross, and follow the Lord. That is what separates spiritual economy seats from first class. Fasting is one of many ways through which we can deny ourselves and pick up our cross. At first, when you're paying the price, it feels hard and painful, but I want to assure you that behind the price of self-denial is the promise of destiny—a closer, more intimate experience with Jesus, and a divine friendship with Him.

One of my favorite things to do during a fast is to read stories of God's martyrs. I get inspired by their feats of faith and how they were willing to lay down their lives to follow the Lord.

There is a vacant seat in first class waiting for you; are you willing to pay the price?

FLYING FIRST CLASS

O Prayer

God, more than anything, I desire an intimate relationship with You. I want to go further where others are unwilling to go and become a disciple of Yours. Help me to live with eternity on my mind. I want to be willing to surrender everything in this life in order to know You more. Holy Spirit, help me to do so; give me the courage to follow You, no matter the cost.

 Ponder

What is motivating you to keep fasting?

FAST FORWARD

Scriptures to meditate on:

But I discipline my body and bring it into subjection, lest, when I have preached to others, I myself should become disqualified.

1 Corinthians 9:27

I have been crucified with Christ; it is no longer I who live, but Christ lives in me; and the life which I now live in the flesh I live by faith in the Son of God, who loved me and gave Himself for me. I do not set aside the grace of God; for if righteousness comes through the law, then Christ died in vain.

Galatians 2:20-21

I affirm, by the boasting in you which I have in Christ Jesus our Lord, I die daily.

1 Corinthians 15:31

And those who are Christ's have crucified the flesh with its passions and desires. If we live in the Spirit, let us also walk in the Spirit.

Galatians 5:24–25

That you put off, concerning your former conduct, the old man which grows corrupt according to the deceitful lusts, and be renewed in the spirit of your mind, and that you put on the new man which was created according to God, in true righteousness and holiness.

Ephesians 4:22-24

FASTING TIP

Physically, there are incredible cleansing and heart health benefits taking place during a fast. As your BMR lowers, fat in the blood starts to disappear as it's metabolized for energy. This process promotes a healthy heart, and for some, improves cholesterol levels by boosting HDL levels. [1]

DAY SEVEN

BOWL FOR BLESSING

> And Jacob gave Esau bread and stew of lentils; then he ate and drank, arose, and went his way. Thus Esau despised his birthright.
>
> Genesis 25:34

Nobody likes to be tricked. When my iPhone 6 stopped working, I decided to upgrade to a newer model. Since money was an issue, I started looking on Craigslist and I found a person who was selling an iPhone 7 for $140. A brand-new phone, and so cheap! I could hardly believe it, so I went to meet the person and buy the phone. I checked it over, but something seemed fishy. The way the phone felt in my hand was odd, and the software looked weird on the inside. But my urgent desire for a new phone and the need to replace my old one made me think that I was simply overreacting. The person selling the phone reassured me that the phone could be wiped, and it would be as good as new on the inside.

I went home happy, excited to get my new phone

set up. There was just one problem: the phone didn't work, didn't call, didn't text or charge, and it couldn't be wiped or restored to factory settings. It was not an iPhone. It was a fake phone with an iPhone cover. I was tricked into getting a counterfeit phone. I paid $140 for a piece of junk in a useless metal iPhone case. I still have that phone in my office as a reminder that not everything that feels and looks real is actually real.

It's not that the person stole my $140; it's that the thing he gave me didn't actually cost $140. That is what happened to Esau. He traded his birthright for a bowl of stew. He got tricked. He fell for it because he considered his physical needs to be more important than his inheritance. The "birthright" was a guarantee that the oldest son would inherit twice as much as his other male siblings. But there was an urgency because he was "famished."

Many people give up the spiritual for the physical, the important for the urgent. I believe that's what happens when the Lord leads us to fast and we refuse to do so. We consider physical nourishment of more value than spiritual blessings. These decisions have sad, disappointing endings: *"When Esau heard the words of his father, he cried with an exceedingly great and bitter cry, and said to his father, "Bless me—me also, O my father!"* (Genesis 27:34). That soup was tasty and satisfying for the moment, but the results were bitter. All Esau had to do that day was fast and do without food. His birthright would have been securely his if he had opted to fast first and eat later.

I wonder how many believers can't access their

BOWL FOR BLESSING

divine inheritance because they refuse to fast. They are driven by physical appetites, and then they wonder why they don't have a spiritual hunger for God. Every time God prompts them to fast, they ignore it until God no longer speaks to them about it. If you want to last, you have to fast. If you want to walk in and enjoy your spiritual inheritance, learn to bridle your physical appetites and tolerate hunger for His sake.

Esau needed to fast to maintain his birthright. Jacob fasted to get the birthright. How did he do it? Jacob exchanged his meal for a blessing. He traded a bowl of food for the first-born's blessing. He got the better end of the stick. That's a great deal. And that's what really happens when we fast—we give up our bowl of food for the blessing of God. We trade the physical for the spiritual, temporary for eternal, natural for the supernatural. It is an amazing trade. It might feel painful at first because we have to put off a plate(s) of food for a season, but it has amazing results. Jacob claimed that blessing as his own, and later the Lord released the full blessing upon him. The rest is history.

Maybe, like Jacob, you feel like you were born on the wrong side of the tracks. You don't have many blessings in your life. Learn the trade of fasting. Embrace the lifestyle of consecration. Give up what is good for the benefit of receiving what is best. Give up your bowl for the blessing.

FAST FORWARD

○ *Prayer*

God, thank You for helping me understand what You desire to give me through this fast. I choose to remain faithful amidst my physical hunger, and to trade what is temporary for what I know is eternal. I pray that You would release Your blessing upon my life in ways I can't even imagine.

 Ponder

What blessings have you already received since you started this fast?

BOWL FOR BLESSING

Scriptures to meditate on:

And Jacob gave Esau bread and stew of lentils; then he ate and drank, arose, and went his way. Thus Esau despised his birthright.

Genesis 25:34

For you know that afterward, when he wanted to inherit the blessing, he was rejected, for he found no place for repentance, though he sought it diligently with tears.

Hebrews 12:17

When Esau heard the words of his father, he cried with an exceedingly great and bitter cry, and said to his father, "Bless me—me also, O my father!"

Genesis 27:34

Jesus said to him, "If you want to be perfect, go, sell what you have and give to the poor, and you will have treasure in heaven; and come, follow Me." But when the young man heard that saying, he went away sorrowful, for he had great possessions.

Matthew 19:21–22

FASTING TIP

Glucose is the primary source of energy for the body. However, when you fast or go into ketosis, glucose becomes limited, and your body must turn to fat stores for the energy it requires. Additionally, getting rid of that extra fat has a detoxifying effect on the body. [1]

DAY EIGHT

FASTING IS FEASTING

> But He answered and said, "It is written, Man shall not live by bread alone, but by every word that proceeds from the mouth of God.'"
>
> Matthew 4:4

When I am fasting, the Lord reminds me that my body's hunger is what my spirit feels when I am not feeding on spiritual food. It is like the Holy Spirit is saying: Finally, you can feel in your body what your real inward man is feeling when he's deprived of nourishment. What sandwiches and roast beef are to my body, the Scriptures are to my spirit. What coffee or tea is to my body, sweet communion with the Holy Spirit is to my spirit.

Hunger and thirst are normal signs of life, and so it is with our spirit—spiritual hunger and thirst are both natural if there is spiritual life within. When a person has no hunger, it's a sign that he is either sick, dead, or dying. It's not normal! Therefore, food and drink for our spirit are not optional; they are a necessity. It's not just for super Christians—it's for everyone. David said, *"My soul thirsts for God"* (Psalm 42:2). The Lord Jesus said, *"Blessed are those who hunger and thirst for righteousness"* (Matthew 5:6). Your spirit gets hungry and thirsty when it is not being fed daily. Fasting helps you to realize what your spirit feels when you are not eating spiritual food for days and weeks.

Humanity's first temptation in the garden was with food. Jesus's first temptation in the wilderness was with food. Israel's first temptation in the desert was with water and food. It is interesting that God took Israel through fasting right after their deliverance from Egypt. Scripture says, *"So He humbled you, allowed you to hunger, and fed you with manna which you did not know nor did your fathers know, that He might make you know that man shall not live by bread alone; but man lives by every word that proceeds from the mouth of the Lord"* (Deuteronomy 8:3). God let Israel hunger so He could feed them with His Word. Fasting reminded them that there is more to being a human being than just feeding their bodies. There is a spiritual part in us that gets hungry and needs food as well. That food is the Word of God, and that is why the Word of God is called bread.

Unfortunately, Israel did not learn this truth in the wilderness. They complained instead of feeding their spirit. They questioned God's faithfulness instead of feasting on His promises. They failed to feed the most important part of who they were: the spiritual part. Therefore, fasting for them was simply a negative and miserable starvation experience. Both their bodies and spirits fasted. When the body was

FASTING IS FEASTING

fasting, the spirit should have been *feasting*.

This is not to say that the only time we are to feed our spirit is when we don't feed our body. But fasting seasons are important because they reset our understanding of who we really are. We are not a body who has a spirit; we are spirits who have a soul and live in a body. If we neglect this truth, we face the danger of being ruled by our senses, feelings, and emotions instead of being led by our inner spirit—dominated by biology instead of theology.

I love how Jesus used the illustration in Matthew 4:4 of when the devil tempted Israel in the desert. He quoted the very same verse that described Israel's time of fasting when they had not yet learned to feast on God's Word. "Man shall not live by bread alone" means that there is more to us than just a physical body. Peter also said we need spiritual food: *"Like newborn babies, crave pure spiritual milk, so that by it you may grow up in your salvation, now that you have tasted that the Lord is good"* (1 Peter 2:2-3 NIV). Because we are spirits, we live by every word that proceeds from the mouth of God. So, when your body is fasting, the real you is not fasting. The real you is feasting, because the real you is your spirit. Give your spirit a feast by consuming God's Word.

When the devil tempted Eve, it was with the only food that God prohibited. Part of the temptation in the garden was an attack on God's Word and authority: And he said to the woman, *"Has God indeed said, 'You shall not eat of every tree of the garden'?"* (Genesis 3:1). That temptation had very little to do with food; it had to do with Eve respecting God's Word.

FAST FORWARD

The devil cannot defeat us until he disarms us, and his best tactic to do so is to either make us doubt God's Word, ignore it, or block His Word from our mind. Jesus warned us about what happens when we disregard God's words: *"When anyone hears the word of the kingdom, and does not understand it, then the wicked one comes and snatches away what was sown in his heart"* (Matthew 13:19). Adam and Eve were instructed to fast, abstain, resist the fruit hanging on the tree of the knowledge of good and evil. All they had to do were to eat from the tree of life. All they needed to do were to feed on God's life-giving Word.

My friend, fasting is more about feasting on spiritual food and less about abstaining from physical food. It serves as a great reminder that we are spirits who need spiritual nourishment every day. Therefore, don't think you're fasting if you're simply abstaining from food. That's called a diet or starvation. Real spiritual fasting is feasting on God's Word while you're taking a temporary pause from physical food.

When you fast, replace your normal eating habits with the reading of God's Word, meditation, memorization of Scriptures, and prayer. Stop all entertainment and unnecessary activities and fill yourself with edifying things that will nourish your spirit. Drink deeply from the rivers of the Holy Spirit.

FASTING IS FEASTING

○ Prayer

Holy Spirit, as I fast, help me fall in love with You in a way I have yet to experience. Help me feed on the Scriptures and not just read them. I desire to find the riches in Your Word. Please make the Scriptures come alive for me. I want to fall in love with Your Word and drink deeply from Your river of living water.

What Scripture has been on your heart lately? What is God telling you through it?

FAST FORWARD

Scriptures to meditate on:

1
Now the serpent was more cunning than any beast of the field which the Lord God had made. And he said to the woman, "Has God indeed said, 'You shall not eat of every tree of the garden'?"

Genesis 3:1

2
But He answered and said, "It is written, 'Man shall not live by bread alone, but by every word that proceeds from the mouth of God.'"

Matthew 4:4

3
And the children of Israel said to them, "Oh, that we had died by the hand of the Lord in the land of Egypt, when we sat by the pots of meat and when we ate bread to the full! For you have brought us out into this wilderness to kill this whole assembly with hunger."

Exodus 16:3

FASTING IS FEASTING

4 So He humbled you, allowed you to hunger, and fed you with manna which you did not know nor did your fathers know, that He might make you know that man shall not live by bread alone; but man lives by every word that proceeds from the mouth of the LORD.

Deuteronomy 8:3

5 As the deer pants for the water brooks, so pants my soul for You, O God. My soul thirsts for God, for the living God. When shall I come and appear before God?

Psalm 42:1-2

6 Blessed are those who hunger and thirst for righteousness, for they shall be filled.

Matthew 5:6

7 And Jesus said to them, "I am the bread of life. He who comes to Me shall never hunger, and he who believes in Me shall never thirst.

John 6:35

FASTING TIP

During stage one and two of the fast, your body will still be expelling toxins and damaged cells every time you go to the bathroom. Using an intestinal cleansing product will help more thoroughly cleanse and detoxify your body. [1]

DAY NINE

WEIGHT, NOT WORTH

> I beseech you therefore, brethren, by the mercies of God, that you present your bodies a living sacrifice, holy, acceptable to God, which is your reasonable service.
>
> Romans 12:1

Before I got married, I weighed 130 pounds, and no matter what I ate I didn't gain any weight. It probably had to do with my rapid metabolism and the lifestyle of exercise that I maintained. Being skinny doesn't mean you are healthy, but being overweight is not good for your health, either. Our body is the means we use to accomplish God's will here on this earth.

However, when I got married, I started to gain weight—very quickly, in fact. At one point, my pastor told me I was growing in my belly more than in my spirit. He told my wife that. Ouch! That hurt my feelings. That night, I began to run in order to lose some weight. I began to watch what I ate. Even though physical activity is not as beneficial as exercising godliness, taking care of our bodies through proper eating, sleep, and exercise shows that we really care about God's temple.

As a side note, fasting is not a solution for controlling a weight issue. You cannot eat like a pig for months and then fast for a few weeks, hoping to undo the consequences of bad eating habits. Good health requires good choices before and after fasting. I know many people who lose a lot of weight while fasting, only to gain it all back and even more after finishing their fast. It is because they don't change their lifestyle.

Now, fasting does not improve our spiritual worth even though it increases our spiritual weight. Paul tells the Romans to *"present your bodies a living sacrifice, holy, acceptable to God, which is your reasonable service"* (Romans 12:1). There are many ways you can do so, and one of them is fasting. Presenting your body as a sacrifice comes before renewing your mind. This sacrifice of the body in service to God comes as a response to God's infinite mercy. That's how Paul starts the chapter:

> *"I beseech you therefore, brethren, by the mercies of God, that you present your bodies a living sacrifice, holy, acceptable to God, which is your reasonable service... be transformed by the renewing of your mind"* (Romans 12:1–2).

For the eleven chapters prior to this, Paul talks about God's grace and mercy through which we obtained salvation. Now in the twelfth chapter, he tells us what our response should be: offer our bodies as a sacrifice, renew our minds, and be transformed.

WEIGHT, NOT WORTH

Fasting is an act of offering our bodies as a living sacrifice. It is a rational response to God's mercy—not an attempt to receive it. Therefore, fasting does not increase our spiritual worth. Our value in God's eyes is fixed by the price His Son Jesus Christ paid on the cross at Calvary. We are not loved more because we fast and pray; we fast and pray because we are loved. We don't read the Bible so God will love us more; we read the Bible to know more about the infinite love that God has for us. This is huge.

Sacrificial living is a response to the sacrifice of Jesus on the cross for us. It is our rational response to His grace, not our attempt to earn that grace.

FAST FORWARD

○ Prayer

Lord, thank You for everything You did for me on the cross. I understand that it was Your love for me that took You to that cross. I pray that You would help me die to myself that You may live through me. And that through this act of fasting, Your love will flow out of me in greater measure and others will come to know You.

✷ Ponder

How is your spirit feeling today?

WEIGHT, NOT WORTH

Scriptures to meditate on:

1
I beseech you therefore, brethren, by the mercies of God, that you present your bodies a living sacrifice, holy, acceptable to God, which is your reasonable service. And do not be conformed to this world, but be transformed by the renewing of your mind, that you may prove what is that good and acceptable and perfect will of God.

Romans 12:1–2

2
For God so loved the world that He gave His only begotten Son, that whoever believes in Him should not perish but have everlasting life.

John 3:16

3
For bodily exercise profits a little, but godliness is profitable for all things, having promise of the life that now is and of that which is to come.

1 Timothy 4:8

FASTING TIP

After the first few days, when the hunger disappears, you may begin to notice that you feel more energetic. Perhaps you feel like going for a jog or hitting the gym, but try and refrain from heavy activities at this stage of the fast. Instead, stick to a light walk around your neighborhood or water the plants, etc.

DAY TEN

THE WAY OF HUMILITY

> God resists the proud, but gives grace to the humble. Therefore humble yourselves under the mighty hand of God, that He may exalt you in due time.
>
> 1 Peter 5:5–6

You may have heard the parable about the two ducks and a frog. On a farm, there was a frog and two ducks, and they were great friends. During the hot summer, the pond dried up. The ducks got ready to fly to another place, but they didn't want to leave the frog behind. They came up with a brilliant plan to hold a stick in their bills between them; the frog would hang onto the stick with its mouth, and they would fly him to another place. As they were flying, a farmer in the field noticed these two ducks flying with a frog. "What a great idea," said the farmer. "I wonder who came up with that." "I did," said the frog. Then the frog fell.

The moral of the story: stay humble! Pride comes before a fall. Pride turned an angel into a devil. Billy

FAST FORWARD

Graham once said that the middle letter of the words *sin*, *Lucifer*, and *pride* is the letter *I*. Is *I* in the center of your life and controlling it?

God resists the proud, but gives grace to the humble. Not only that, but He exalts the humble: *"By humility and the fear of the LORD are riches and honor and life"* (Proverbs 22:4). Riches, honor, and life—who doesn't want that? The key is humility! Another proverb says, *"When pride comes, then comes shame; but with the humble is wisdom"* (Proverbs 11:2).

Okay, I get it. Humility is pretty much the essential key to everything in God's kingdom. But humility is not something God will do for us! It is an attribute that we must willingly practice before Him daily ourselves. He tells us to humble ourselves and reflect on His supreme sovereignty, power, and glory.

So how do we become more humble? Fasting is a biblical way of humbling yourself before God. David humbled his soul with fasting: *"When I wept and humbled my soul with fasting, it became my reproach"* (Psalm 69:10 ESV). In another instance, he said, *"I humbled myself with fasting"* (Psalm 35:13).

Ezra humbled himself with fasting as well: *"Then I proclaimed a fast there at the river of Ahava, that we might humble ourselves before our God, to seek from Him the right way for us and our little ones and all our possessions"* (Ezra 8:21).

Even the wicked king Ahab humbled himself by fasting after the prophet Elijah pronounced judgment over him and his descendants: *"So it was, when Ahab heard those words, that he tore his clothes and put sackcloth on his body, and fasted and lay in sackcloth, and went about mourning"* (1 Kings 21:27). Now, look at what God saw: *"See how Ahab has humbled himself before Me? Because he has humbled himself before Me, I will not bring the calamity in his days. In the days of his son I will bring the calamity on his house"* (1 Kings 21:29). Wow—the worst king in Israel's history received God's extended mercy and favor just because he humbled himself through fasting!

If you want to have God's favor, exaltation, honor, abundant life, and spiritual riches in your life, fear the Lord with reverence and humility. One of the best ways you can humble yourself is by fasting.

It is important to not take pride in our fasting, as that defeats its purpose. Fasting should help us to be humble in our hearts, not proud. Bragging and putting your private fasting or the length of it for all to see gets attention from man instead of a reward from God. Your fasting should be for God's attention, but that will never happen if you are doing it to get men's attention. Jesus said, *"your Father who sees in secret will reward you openly"* (Matthew 6:18).

FAST FORWARD

O *Prayer*

Father, forgive me if there was any ulterior motive within my heart motivating this fast. Forgive any prideful behavior and attitude that might be driving my desire to seek You. Purify my heart, wash me, and make me as white as snow.

※ **Ponder**

How are you doing in the area of humility?

THE WAY OF HUMILITY

Scriptures to meditate on:

1
Moreover, when you fast, do not be like the hypocrites, with a sad countenance. For they disfigure their faces that they may appear to men to be fasting. Assuredly, I say to you, they have their reward. But you, when you fast, anoint your head and wash your face, so that you do not appear to men to be fasting, but to your Father who is in the secret place; and your Father who sees in secret will reward you openly.

Matthew 6:16–18

2
Then I proclaimed a fast there at the river of Ahava, that we might humble ourselves before our God, to seek from Him the right way for us and our little ones and all our possessions.

Ezra 8:21

3
But as for me, when they were sick, my clothing was sackcloth; I humbled myself with fasting; and my prayer would return to my own heart.

Psalm 35:13

FAST FORWARD

4 So it was, when Ahab heard those words, that he tore his clothes and put sackcloth on his body, and fasted and lay in sackcloth, and went about mourning. And the word of the Lord came to Elijah the Tishbite, saying, "See how Ahab has humbled himself before Me? Because he has humbled himself before Me, I will not bring the calamity in his days. In the days of his son I will bring the calamity on his house."

1 Kings 21:27–29

5 When pride comes, then comes shame; But with the humble *is* wisdom.

Proverbs 11:2

6 By humility and the fear of the Lord are riches and honor and life.

Proverbs 22:4

7 Likewise you younger people, submit yourselves to your elders. Yes, all of you be submissive to one another, and be clothed with humility, for "God resists the proud, but gives grace to the humble." Therefore humble yourselves under the mighty hand of God, that He may exalt you in due time.

1 Peter 5:5–6

FASTING TIP

Stage three typically falls between day eight and fifteen. This stage includes dramatic improvements in mood and mental clarity and is the stage seasoned fasters look forward to the most. Keep pushing! [1]

DAY ELEVEN

FROM CRISIS TO CALLING

> As they ministered to the Lord and fasted, the Holy Spirit said, "Now separate to me Barnabas and Saul for the work to which I have called them."
>
> Acts 13:2

There was a man who was totally hopeless and despaired of life. His wife had left him, he had lost his job, and he lost the will to live. He decided to end his life by jumping off a bridge. He wrote a note, left it at his residence, and headed to the bridge. He found the best spot to jump, away where no one could see him. He was about to jump when he saw a person drowning in the river below and screaming for help. That frantic cry reached his ears and touched his heart. He quickly ran down from the bridge and swam to the rescue. He saved a girl's life that day. A crowd gathered, her family came, and newspaper reporters arrived. Everyone was so thankful that he was there at the right time and at the right place. Then, they heard his sad story of why he was there on that bridge. The next day, the newspaper printed a front-page article about the event: "A Purpose Saved a Man's Life." It was his life that was saved that day, not just the drowning girl's. Having a purpose is a very powerful motivator.

I find it interesting that most of the fasting recorded in the New Testament was not in response to a problem; it was an essential key to fulfilling a higher purpose. Jesus's forty-day fast was not because of a crisis in His life; it was what catapulted Him into His calling. His ministry on earth started after that fast. The fasting mentioned in Acts 13:2 also was not a response to a problem; it was evidence of their fervent pursuit of God's presence. Many people fast only when they have problems or crises, but God wants us to fast even when we don't have a crisis.

When I was doing my forty-day fast, I didn't have any problems with my health, family, relationships, or finances. My fast was to pursue the Lord with a passion and to humble myself before Him so my life would bring Him the most glory; *"By this My Father is glorified, that you bear much fruit"* (John 15:8).

The real ministry of Jesus started after His forty-day fast. Paul discovered his initial ministry after a three-day fast, but his real calling intensified into a defined ministry after the fast of Acts 13. On the road to Damascus, he encountered the Lord. During that meeting with Jesus, Paul asked Him two questions: "Who are You, Lord?" and, "Lord, what do You want me to do?" I love that! Paul had two great questions. After Jesus revealed Himself to Paul on the road, He told him to go into the city to get further instructions on the second question: *"Then the Lord said to him, 'Arise and go into the city, and you will be told what you must do'"* (Acts 9:6).

During those three days without sight, food, and drink, Paul received another vision of how he was going to receive his sight. The Lord also gave Ananias a vision with specific instructions and a clear picture of what the Lord was calling Paul to do. He was to be a chosen instrument to declare Jesus's name before gentiles, kings, and children of Israel. Now, it seems like that's a worldwide ministry right there. Paul spent the next 17 years (Galatians 1:18, 2:1) learning the Word, teaching, preaching, hanging out with Christians, sharing his faith, and giving money to the poor.

But, after the Acts 13 fast, the Holy Spirit said, *"Separate to me Barnabas and Saul for the work to which I have called them"* (Acts 13:2). Whatever they had been doing before was good, but now they would be stepping into something greater that the Holy Spirit had been preparing them for. There is ministry that we do for the Lord, but when we take time to fast and minister to the Lord, He will empower us to minister in our specific God-given callings. Our ministry *for* the Lord is done in our own strength and understanding; ministry *from* the Lord is done in His might and purpose. The big difference between these two is in our willingness to pause, fast, and minister to the Lord Himself.

In my own ministry, I have experienced how prolonged fasting changes the parameters of my service to the Lord. Fasting takes it to another level, to greater dimensions, and opens doors that only God is able to open. However, fasting is not some kind of gimmick for ministry growth. It is the means to humility that positions one for God's favor. It is the ancient biblical way to get yourself aligned with God's purposes and then operate from His grace, instead of grinding away at your own ministry.

FROM CRISIS TO CALLING

○ Prayer

Lord, I humble my heart before You. I was made for You. Show me where You want me to go; teach me. Guide me toward my purpose as I surrender myself for Your purposes.

✷ Ponder

Have you noticed a shift in any area of my life since you began the fast? If so, in what area(s) and what was the change?

FAST FORWARD

Scriptures to meditate on:

1 Then Jesus returned in the power of the Spirit to Galilee, and news of Him went out through all the surrounding region. And He taught in their synagogues, being glorified by all.

Luke 4:14–15

2 Then after three years I went up to Jerusalem to see Peter, and remained with him fifteen days.

Galatians 1:18

3 Then after fourteen years I went up again to Jerusalem with Barnabas, and also took Titus with *me*.

Galatians 2:1

As they ministered to the Lord and fasted, the Holy Spirit said, "Now separate to Me Barnabas and Saul for the work to which I have called them." Then, having fasted and prayed, and laid hands on them, they sent them away.

Acts 13:2–3

Therefore I remind you to stir up the gift of God which is in you through the laying on of my hands.

2 Timothy 1:6

FASTING TIP

By the third stage, a sort of "fasting high" begins. These improvements include an elevated mood, increased energy levels, and a type of clear mindedness unique to fasting. [1]

DAY TWELVE

THREEFOLD CORD

> Though one may be overpowered by another, two can withstand him. And a threefold cord is not quickly broken.
>
> Acts 13:2

What is a trial? It is a test you go through, helping you to discover your moral qualities or character. However, trial and temptation are not the same. Temptation is a seduction to evil—inclinations to wrong thoughts and actions; temptation entices you to do evil in order to ruin you: *"but each person is tempted when they are dragged away by their own evil desire and enticed"* (James 1:14 NIV). One aims at man's moral good, making him conscious of his true moral self; the other targets his evil tendencies, leading him into sin. "God tries; Satan tempts." [1]

Every temptation that we face on this side of eternity can be traced to the lust of the eyes, the lust of the flesh, or the pride of life (1 John 2:15–16). This is the devil's trio. Our first parents faced these desires in the garden. Satan also attacked Jesus with the same tactic, or strategy, in the wilderness. Whether it be pride, lust, or money—or as someone said, "gold, girls, and greed," all sins fall under these three categories. These are the three types of temptation that we all have to deal with.

Now, for these three temptations, the Lord gave us three weapons. These are clearly presented in Jesus's Sermon on the Mount in Matthew 6, where He teaches us three Christian principles: praying, giving, and fasting. I believe that these three disciplines help combat all the temptations that Satan throws at us.

Prayer fights pride

In fact, prayerlessness is a sign of pride. Pride is always pregnant with other sins, and prayer aborts whatever pride wants to birth. People don't pray much when they are proud. Busyness gets blamed for our lack of prayer, but the real root cause is our pride. We think we can make it without God and that His assistance is unnecessary; we ignore His voice, we often miss His leading, and grieve the Holy Spirit. But sincere prayer removes this carefree, independent attitude. Start a habit of daily repentance before the Lord. Carve out time for prayer, get on your knees, repent of your sins, humble your heart, ask for God's help—then pride cannot take root in your heart. Jesus clarified the purpose of prayer and how to pray. It is powerful when it is done with the right heart posture, and we have our best example in the Lord's Prayer (Matthew 6:9-13).

Giving crushes greed

Greed is not a person acquiring money; it is when money has acquired a person. Greed can attack the poor as well as the rich. It destroyed Achan, Gehazi, Judas, and Ananias. Greed can make you its target as well. There is only one cure for greed, and it is not prayer for deliverance—it's giving! And if you really want to hit greed and pride in the throat, try sacrificial giving. Jesus called it "laying up your treasure in heaven." Giving your treasure to Him is much more than just giving away what you don't need to help poor people or giving God a tip on Sunday. It is giving whatever hurts to give away. That kind of giving redirects your heart toward eternal values. As with prayer, your motives for giving are as important as giving itself.

Fasting hits lust

Lust is about the cravings of the flesh and desires of the body. While fasting, a person voluntarily denies what the body actually needs, thus preparing the body to be controlled by one's spirit. When we discipline our natural physical desires, it becomes easier to control the flesh's evil desires that are sinful. Train the flesh to submit to the spirit through seasons of fasting.

FAST FORWARD

Fasting will prepare you to fight temptation. When we fast, we deny ourselves food, but after fasting we have the willpower to abstain from sin. The flesh always wants to do stupid things, but once you take dominion over it through fasting, it is much easier to control when temptation comes.

One of the first recommendations I give to those battling with lust is to develop a lifestyle of fasting and self-denial. Fasting is like being a boxer who works out at the gym for months before his boxing match. No athlete would think of getting ready for the match when he steps into the ring. That is far too late. Prior to that boxing match, he watches his diet and keeps up with his daily training in the gym, in preparation for that one match. That is what fasting is: a spiritual gym for the flesh, so that when you enter the boxing ring of temptation, you don't get knocked out.

Keep these three spiritual disciplines active in your life: prayer, giving, and fasting. When you go to the gym, you need to work out all the parts of your body. Girls like to work more on legs and guys like to work more on their chest and abs, but really, all parts need to be worked on; otherwise, you would look weird and disproportionate. Our exercise in godliness, prayer, giving, and fasting are not just about our spiritual growth, but about our spiritual victory. Living a life of prayer, giving, and fasting is not optional. It is a must!

---

[1] *The Words and Works of Jesus Christ: a Study of the Life of Christ*, by J. Dwight Pentecost and John Danilson, Zondervan Pub. House, 1984, pp. 99–99.

O *Prayer*

Father, forgive me for any prayerlessness and stinginess that has taken over my heart. Help me to be generous and to develop a love for prayer and for fasting. Remove any pride that has crept its way into my heart. I want to live free from all of that.

What are some areas in your heart that God is working on during this fast?

FAST FORWARD

Scriptures to meditate on:

1 Though one may be overpowered by another, two can withstand him. And a threefold cord is not quickly broken.

Ecclesiastes 4:12

2 But each one is tempted when he is drawn away by his own desires and enticed. Then, when desire has conceived, it gives birth to sin; and sin, when it is full-grown, brings forth death.

James 1:14–15

3 For all that is in the world—the lust of the flesh, the lust of the eyes, and the pride of life—is not of the Father but is of the world. And the world is passing away, and the lust of it; but he who does the will of God abides forever.

1 John 2:16–17

Therefore put to death your members which are on the earth: fornication, uncleanness, passion, evil desire, and covetousness, which is idolatry.

Colossians 3:5

So when the woman saw that the tree was good for food, that it was pleasant to the eyes, and a tree desirable to make one wise, she took of its fruit and ate. She also gave to her husband with her, and he ate.

Genesis 3:6

Look, this was the iniquity of your sister Sodom: She and her daughter had pride, fullness of food, and abundance of idleness; neither did she strengthen the hand of the poor and needy.

Ezekiel 16:49

FAST FORWARD

Now when the tempter came to Him, he said, "If You are the Son of God, command that these stones become bread." But He answered and said, "It is written, 'Man shall not live by bread alone, but by every word that proceeds from the mouth of God.'" Then the devil took Him up into the holy city, set Him on the pinnacle of the temple, and said to Him, "If You are the Son of God, throw Yourself down. For it is written: 'He shall give His angels charge over you,' and, 'In their hands they shall bear you up, lest you dash your foot against a stone.'" Jesus said to him, "It is written again, 'You shall not tempt the Lord your God.'" Again, the devil took Him up on an exceedingly high mountain, and showed Him all the kingdoms of the world and their glory. And he said to Him, "All these things I will give You if You will fall down and worship me."

Matthew 4:3–9

FASTING TIP

During stage three, your body starts to enter into a "healing mode." This healing process begins as your digestive system takes a rest from the common stressors and toxins it endures on a daily basis. As a result, your body has fewer free radicals entering the mix, and oxidative stress decreases. [1]

DAY THIRTEEN

BUILDING, BINDING, AND BIRTHING

> So Cornelius said, "Four days ago I was fasting until this hour; and at the ninth hour I prayed in my house, and behold, a man stood before me in bright clothing, and said, 'Cornelius, your prayer has been heard, and your alms are remembered in the sight of God'."
>
> Acts 10:30–31

The discipline of prayer, fasting, and giving has a powerful effect on our spiritual development. When combined, they yield the powerful fruit of godliness for the glory of God.

Solomon said, *"Though one may be overpowered by another, two can withstand him. And a threefold cord is not quickly broken"* (Ecclesiastes 4:12). As believers, we have a tendency to highlight one discipline above another. Some minimize fasting because they are so focused on giving or praying. Others only fast and do not develop a generous lifestyle of giving. These three must go together.

FAST FORWARD

Cornelius lived a life of prayer, fasting, and giving. It attracted God's attention, but it didn't bring him salvation. Salvation comes by grace through faith (Ephesians 2:8-9). It is fascinating that he lived a godly lifestyle even before being saved. Many saved folks today only come to the cross but never take up their cross to die to themselves. They receive salvation, but they aren't allowing the Holy Spirit to bring forth sanctification by means of the cross. So please be aware that fasting is not a method to improve our standing with God or earn our salvation, but the means of self-denial.

Prayer, fasting, and giving builds our inner man. By spending time with God, voluntarily setting aside food, and giving of our resources, we increase our sensitivity to the Lord and His awesome character. When we are born again, our spirit is made alive and perfect before God. The author of Hebrews says, *"For by one offering He has perfected forever those who are being sanctified"* (Hebrews 10:14). Our spiritual man, though perfect, must grow into maturity—even Jesus went through it: *"And the Child [Jesus] grew and became strong in spirit, filled with wisdom; and the grace of God was upon Him"* (Luke 2:40). Even though a healthy baby is considered perfect in the eyes of his parents, it must eat and drink to grow into a mature adult. *"As newborn babes, desire the pure milk of the word, that you may grow thereby"* (1 Peter 2:2). Obedience to God brings growth to our spiritual man. Abiding in God's Word, talking to God in prayer, fasting, and giving are all necessary tools to grow the spiritual man.

BUILDING, BINDING, AND BIRTHING

Prayer, fasting, and giving subdue the flesh. (Please understand, your body and your flesh are not the same. During a fast our body gets healthier, and our flesh and its sinful desires get mortified). Our three chief enemies are the world, the flesh, and the devil. The world is the outward enemy, the flesh is the inward enemy, and the devil is the invisible enemy. Fasting helps us to put our flesh under the subjection of our spirit. The flesh is the devil's "gift" on your birthday, and you can't get rid of it. It is inborn; you can't get it cast out of you with a prayer for deliverance. The only remedy against the flesh is the cross, or in other words, death; self-denial. Paul said, "... *I die daily"* (1 Corinthians 15:31), meaning to the flesh. As I mentioned before, prayer helps to beat down pride, fasting delivers a blow to lust, and giving smashes greed. Many believers start with binding the devil before they are successful in subduing the flesh. You must conquer your lions and bears before you embark on the conquest of giants.

Prayer, fasting, and giving will *birth breakthrough*. Cornelius was doing all these things on a regular basis and *then* the angel showed up with clear instructions on what to do next. His faith was never again the same. Cornelius was the first gentile (non-Jew) convert, and God divinely connected him to Peter. In fact, God gave a vision to Peter as he was praying and fasting while in another city; Cornelius was also praying and fasting. God divinely connected two people who were fasting.

When we humble ourselves, God will bring divine encounters into our lives. Everyone wants divine connections in their life, ministry, and career. God is

FAST FORWARD

interested in bringing people together. God is in a good mood, wanting to birth something in you and through your life that will affect your family, community, and region. I encourage you to search your heart to get rid of your pride and ego, get on your knees, push away the plate, and smash the idol of materialism.

BUILDING, BINDING, AND BIRTHING

⭕ Prayer

Jesus, I desire to take up my cross and follow You. Help me to break down my pride, my stubbornness, and any fleshly desire that I might want more than Your will. During this fast, build my inner man. Strengthen me and build me into the child You created me to be. Align me to Your will and help me to rise up and follow You.

✷ Ponder

Is there a new vision, or perhaps a revived dream, that God reminded or has planted in your heart during this fast?

FAST FORWARD

Scriptures to meditate on:

1

Then Jesus said to His disciples, "If anyone desires to come after Me, let him deny himself, and take up his cross, and follow Me."

Matthew 16:24

2

As newborn babes, desire the pure milk of the word, that you may grow thereby.

1 Peter 2:2

3

And the Child grew and became strong in spirit, filled with wisdom; and the grace of God was upon Him.

Luke 2:40

FASTING TIP

Fasting also causes stress that provides added benefit. This is a kind of mild stress that is comparable to the stress caused by exercise, which ultimately makes you stronger and your immune system more resilient. [1]

DAY FOURTEEN

FAST TO GET FIRST LOVE

> But the days will come when the bridegroom will be taken away from them; then they will fast in those days.
>
> Luke 5:35

I remember when I first met Lana. We had already been talking on Facebook and Skype for a few weeks. That day I was preaching in a Messianic church in Vancouver, and I invited her to come. After the service, the church had a little potluck dinner and we had a chance to sit, chat, and eat. I was mesmerized by her—smitten by her beauty and captivated by her personality. She was shy yet confident. A week later, she invited me to dinner at her house. Everything about her was perfect. I was in love. Those feelings were so strong that I wanted to get married the next day. I knew I had found what I was looking for.

Those strong emotions highlighted our decisions until we got married. After marriage, our love for each other produced emotions even deeper than those of couples who are only dating. And now that we have been married for 11 years, my feelings for her are even stronger today than they were in those early days.

Feelings of infatuation don't require any intentional sacrifice. That's what falling in love is; you simply fall. But marriage cannot be built on that. Love is not a valley you fall into; it is a path you walk on: *"Walk in love, as Christ also has loved us and given Himself for us"* (Ephesians 5:2). If you only fall into love, you will soon fall out of love. The love that I feel today for my wife is based on a decision, a personal choice, a commitment. It is not something that controls me, it is something that I choose. Choices should lead, and feelings will follow.

It is the same with our relationship with the Lord. The love that we feel when we first get saved—the hunger for His Word, the thirst for His presence—is incredible. But many of us, like the church of Ephesus in the book of Revelation, lose our first love. This church did not lack good works, labor, patience, or perseverance. Jesus even commended them! They *"labored for My name's sake and have not become weary"* (Revelation 2:3). They worked hard for the Lord. But they neglected the Lord Himself! In the next verse, Jesus gives a loving rebuke: *"Nevertheless I have this against you, that you have left your first love"* (v. 4). That hunger, passion, longing, and thirst for the Lord was missing. Distraction crept in. Stagnation settled in. The church became complacent. They got so comfortable with the things of God that they lost their fascination for God Himself. Now what?

Jesus outlined the process of returning to their first love: *"Remember therefore from where you have fallen; repent and do the first works"* (Revelation 2:5).

Remember, repent, and repeat the first works. These are three simple steps to coming back to your first love. It all starts with remembering and reflecting on how things were at first. Then repent, which is a change of mind that results in a change of direction. After repentance, choose to become zealous again in doing the first works. This is how to regain your first love: Jesus.

If you don't make these adjustments to come back to the Lord, this consequence follows: *"Or else I will come to you quickly and remove your lampstand from its place—unless you repent"* (Revelation 2:5). The consequence was that their lampstand would be removed from its place. A lamp provides light in the dark. It is as though Jesus was saying to them (us), *You will lose your influence in the dark spiritual world.* You will no longer have spiritual authority nor walk in God's anointing unless you reflect, repent, and return.

When we start to *remember, repent,* and *repeat the first works,* our first love returns. When we lay our flesh on the altar, our first love comes back. Strong feelings for the Lord accompany our decisions of consecration and sacrifice. Make these sacrifices and the fire will return.

Jesus told the Pharisees that once the bridegroom is taken away, then His disciples would fast. Now we know that this refers to Jesus's ascension, but the practical application can be for us today as well. Anytime the presence of God seems to be distant in our life, we should fast. When the manifest presence of the Holy Spirit seems to be distant, we should fast.

FAST FORWARD

Fasting helps to restore our hunger, our passion, and our first love.

FAST TO GET FIRST LOVE

O Prayer

Lord, thank You for Your relentless love toward me. I am sorry for being so easily distracted by the things of this world that my love for You fluctuates. Bring to my mind the things that have so easily settled in my heart and have cooled my love for You. I repent of that sin. I want to love You more deeply still. Please teach me how.

✵ Ponder

How would you currently describe your relationship with the Lord? Do you spend quiet time with Him, heart to heart?

FAST FORWARD

Scriptures to meditate on:

1
"To the angel of the church of Ephesus write, 'These things says He who holds the seven stars in His right hand, who walks in the midst of the seven golden lampstands: "I know your works, your labor, your patience, and that you cannot bear those who are evil. And you have tested those who say they are apostles and are not, and have found them liars; and you have persevered and have patience, and have labored for My name's sake and have not become weary. Nevertheless I have this against you, that you have left your first love. Remember therefore from where you have fallen; repent and do the first works, or else I will come to you quickly and remove your lampstand from its place—unless you repent.'"

Revelation 2:1–5

2
But the days will come when the bridegroom will be taken away from them; then they will fast in those days.

Luke 5:35

3
And walk in love, as Christ also has loved us and given Himself for us, an offering and a sacrifice to God for a sweet-smelling aroma.

Ephesians 5:2

> Anytime you limit free radicals and oxidative stress, you are encouraging healthy aging and positioning yourself for fewer health complications. [1]

DAY FIFTEEN

PRIVATE DISCIPLINE, PUBLIC REWARD

> So that you do not appear to men to be fasting, but to your Father who is in the secret place; and your Father who sees in secret will reward you openly.
>
> Luke 5:35

As a kid growing up with four siblings in Ukraine, we loved to pull out all the toys we had and play together. That's why our house would quite often be a mess. We would turn the whole place upside down. Sometimes we played war in the house; other times, we played church. Sometimes, war and church were the same game! As long as we cleaned the house at the end of the day, we were good. But sometimes we would get unexpected visitors who came unannounced, and our parents gave us only a few minutes to clean up the mess we had made.

Being the oldest, I was put in charge of speed cleaning. My siblings and I developed a trick that worked every time: instead of putting everything where it belonged, we would push things under the bed, behind the couch, and in the closet to make the house look spotless in minutes. There was just one problem: if anyone were to check under the bed or behind the couch, or by accident open the closet door, they would be shocked by all the things that were stuffed in there. While guests were impressed with the tidy house, we knew that nothing was really cleaned up—it was simply hidden.

I wonder if that is what Jesus had against religious people who focused on cleaning the outside of the cup while they left the inside dirty. They tried to make themselves look good to people instead of making sure they were good with God. God dwells in the secret place, and He sees what is done in secret. In other words, God sees behind the couch, under the bed, and in the closet. He is present in places we tend to neglect. In our attempt to please men, we decorate our outside to look good and ignore the cluttered inside.

Fasting is a private discipline that brings public reward. God Himself promised to reward you openly when you fast properly. The devil causes people to sin privately, but God teaches us to separate ourselves privately. Whatever we do in private will be seen in public; it's only a matter of time.

There are two stories that happened simultaneously in the Book of Joshua: the story of Achan and the story of Rahab. While their stories happen in the same place and time, these two individuals couldn't be more different from each other. Both were covering or hiding something, but *what* they were hiding forever changed their destinies.

PRIVATE DISCIPLINE, PUBLIC REWARD

Achan
was a soldier

Rahab
was a prostitute

Achan
had a promising future

Rahab
faced a certain doom

Achan
*was hiding **something*** ◀ ▶ Rahab
*was hiding **someone***

Achan's
actions destroyed his family

Rahab's
actions saved her family

Achan
*brought defeat to
God's nation*

Rahab
*became a part of the
God's nation*

FAST FORWARD

Whatever is done in private will be rewarded in public. For Achan, his secret sin resulted in a public scandal and national defeat. For Rahab, her private act of courage resulted in public reward. It changed her family tree; she was not only saved, but she also became an ancestor of king David and of Jesus Christ. Our Heavenly Father sees what is done in private.

Now, we are not in a position today to hide Israeli spies, but we are in a position to do something that can attract the same attention from God as Rahab did. Fasting, when done with the right attitude, that is to get God's attention, will result in getting the Father's reward.

Maybe today your life is headed in the wrong direction, perhaps you are stagnant in your career, or you feel lukewarm in your spiritual life, maybe your family isn't serving the Lord, or your marriage is hanging by a thread. Rahab was really in a bad place—her life was a mess. And yet, her act of faith in the God of Israel and hiding the spies turned that all around.

God is looking at your personal life today. He sees what is in your closet, under the bed, and behind the couch. And He is looking for something to reward you with publicly. *"For the eyes of the LORD run to and fro throughout the whole earth, to show Himself strong on behalf of those whose heart is loyal to Him."* (2 Chronicles 16:9). Will He find something in your secret place that will be worth rewarding you publicly for? Are you quietly fasting? Live in a secret place of prayer, fasting, and giving, and your Father in heaven will bless you and reward you.

PRIVATE DISCIPLINE, PUBLIC REWARD

O *Prayer*

God, I thank You for Your goodness and Your mercy. I pray that You would search me and create a clean heart within me. I repent if I have not stored Your Word in my heart as I should. Teach me to honor You in private through my daily devotion to You. Help me to live in constant awareness that everything I do in private will be shown in public.

✷ *Ponder*

Through reflection, what do you think could be hiding in your heart that God either wants to bring forth or eliminate?

FAST FORWARD

Scriptures to meditate on:

1
"Woe to you, scribes and Pharisees, hypocrites! For you cleanse the outside of the cup and dish, but inside they are full of extortion and self-indulgence. Blind Pharisee, first cleanse the inside of the cup and dish, that the outside of them may be clean also. "Woe to you, scribes and Pharisees, hypocrites! For you are like whitewashed tombs which indeed appear beautiful outwardly, but inside are full of dead men's bones and all uncleanness. Even so you also outwardly appear righteous to men, but inside you are full of hypocrisy and lawlessness."

Matthew 23:25–28

2
For nothing is secret that will not be revealed, nor anything hidden that will not be known and come to light.

Luke 8:17

3
But without faith it is impossible to please Him, for he who comes to God must believe that He is, and that He is a rewarder of those who diligently seek Him.

Hebrews 11:6

Fasting can be great for the liver; when your body isn't being bombarded with salts, colorants, sugars, and artificial chemicals, it gets a chance to rest – and your body gets a chance to process all of the harmful chemicals. [2]

FASTING TIP

DAY SIXTEEN

GO DEEPER

> When He had stopped speaking, He said to Simon, "Launch out into the deep and let down your nets for a catch."
>
> Luke 5:4

We get very strong winds in the Tri-Cities where I live. One time, during a windstorm, a tree close to our church toppled over. The tree fell down like a pencil balanced on its tip. The roots were totally exposed, and although they were very thick, they were surprisingly shallow. The tree was big, but the roots were small; therefore, the wind was able to knock it down from its standing position. This is exactly what happens to us when our public life is more notable than our private life.

Every tree has branches that produce leaves and fruit, and a root system that supports the weight of the tree. Roots are not usually visible; they are underground. And so it is with our life. We have branches—responsibilities which increase with time. The responsibilities that I had when I was sixteen years old are totally different from the responsibilities I have today at the age of thirty-five. At sixteen, I was expected to bring home good grades, clean my room, wash my car, and preach at the youth group meeting on Thursdays. As the years passed, my branches grew; my tasks increased, my plate got bigger, and my weight got heavier. Today I have more people on my staff than I had in my youth group nineteen years ago. This is our dilemma, me included: sometimes the branches keep growing, but the roots don't. Responsibilities and voluntary services increase with time, and it is essential that our relationship with God grows proportionally. Otherwise, what happened to the tree next to our church will happen to us. The branches outgrew the roots. Responsibilities can outgrow relationship.

What does it mean to grow deeper? Does it mean to pray more or fast more or give more? Something the Lord impressed on my heart once during my prayer time answered that question for me. When roots of a tree go deeper, they grow deeper into the ground. To go deep is to go low. There is one key, and it is not more time in prayer and the Bible. It's not even more time spent fasting. It's humility—a modest view of one's importance. Let God do the lifting: *"Humble yourselves in the sight of the Lord, and He will lift you up"* (James 4:10). Humility will result in prayer and fasting. Humility is the key to sustained personal revival. You can be a part of public revival and have a private ruin. You can be in a church that has momentum and be miserable. Your roots are too shallow. The weight of the influence has outgrown the depth of your intimacy. The branches have become too big and heavy for your root system to sustain. You must go deeper into the soil of God's presence and Word. To go deeper, you must intensify your dependence on the Holy Spirit. To go deeper, you must go lower.

When the disciples didn't catch fish all night, discouraged from their failed attempt at fishing, they decided to clean the nets. In the meantime, they let Jesus use their boat to preach to the masses. But Jesus wanted to do more than just use their boat; He wanted to fill it with fish. However, there was a catch to the miracle catch: they had to launch out into the deep.

If you are disappointed with the lack of fruit in your ministry or success in your life, launch into the deep. Deepen your roots in God. Humble yourself before Him. Take care of your private life. Give heed to your thought life. Strip yourself of self-confidence and cast yourself on the goodness and mercy of God. That is the depth that is a result of dependence on the Lord. This humility brings about God's favor and grace. A miracle catch is waiting for you in the deep. Leave the shallow waters of pleasing man and live for the audience of One. Give God something in your private life for Him to reward you publicly.

That is really the heart of fasting; it is humbling ourselves before Almighty God to seek His favor and mercy. Once we move our boats from the shallow religious shores into the depths of greater dependence on Him, we will be ready to encounter His miracle catch.

FAST FORWARD

○ *Prayer*

Holy Spirit, there is nothing I can hide from You. You see my heart's condition and the roots that have grown over time. I pray that You would help me to go deeper in my relationship with You. I no longer want to live in the shallow end, that I have grown accustomed to. I want every day to be a new experience with You. Help me live a life of full surrender and following You wherever You take me. I humble myself before You.

✺ *Ponder*

How has the Lord been directing you to "go deeper" in the past few days? Is there any area in your heart that you feel He is addressing?

GO DEEPER

Scriptures to meditate on:

When He had stopped speaking, He said to Simon, "Launch out into the deep and let down your nets for a catch."

Luke 5:4

Thus says the Lord: "Cursed is the man who trusts in man and makes flesh his strength, whose heart departs from the Lord. For he shall be like a shrub in the desert, and shall not see when good comes, but shall inhabit the parched places in the wilderness, in a salt land which is not inhabited. "Blessed is the man who trusts in the Lord, and whose hope is the Lord. For he shall be like a tree planted by the waters, which spreads out its roots by the river, and will not fear when heat comes; but its leaf will be green, and will not be anxious in the year of drought, nor will cease from yielding fruit. "The heart is deceitful above all things, and desperately wicked; who can know it?"

Jeremiah 17:5-9

Humble yourselves in the sight of the Lord, and He will lift you up.

James 4:10

FAST FORWARD

He shall be like a tree planted by the rivers of water, that brings forth its fruit in its season, whose leaf also shall not wither; and whatever he does shall prosper.

Psalm 1:3

To console those who mourn in Zion, to give them beauty for ashes, the oil of joy for mourning, the garment of praise for the spirit of heaviness; that they may be called trees of righteousness, the planting of the Lord, that He may be glorified.

Isaiah 61:3

But I am like a green olive tree in the house of God; I trust in the mercy of God forever and ever.

Psalm 52:8

FASTING TIP

Fasting puts your body through a rejuvenating experience. It dissolves diseased cells, leaving only healthy tissue. There's also a noticeable redistribution of nutrients in the body. The body hangs onto precious vitamins and minerals while processing and getting rid of old tissue, toxins, or undesirable materials. [3]

DAY SEVENTEEN

GOLD, SILVER, AND PRECIOUS STONES

> Now if anyone builds on this foundation with gold, silver, precious stones, wood, hay, straw...
>
> 1 Corinthians 3:12

In his letter to the Christians in Corinth, the apostle Paul exhorted us to build our spiritual houses with Jesus Christ as its foundation; using gold, silver, and precious stones as building material. That way, on the Day of Judgment our work will endure and we will receive our reward. However, if we build with wood, hay, and straw, then fire will burn it and we will suffer loss, even though we will be saved in the end.

Gold, silver, and precious stones are all hidden underground. They are expensive, rare, usually come in small quantities, and are purified by fire. The life that Paul speaks of is more than just not sinning and living a busy, productive life. It is about paying the price of prioritizing our relationship with the Holy Spirit in private. It is about personal disciplines like fasting, prayer, and sacrifice.

FAST FORWARD

Gold represents prayer. In the book of Revelation, the Bible describes golden bowls full of incense as prayers of the saints (Revelation 5:8). As gold, our prayers are valuable.

Silver represents fasting. David says that God has tested us as silver is refined (Psalm 66:10). A time of fasting is a time of refining our motives and attitudes.

Precious stones represent sacrificial giving. God refers to His people as precious jewels (Malachi 3:16–17; Zechariah 9:16). Sacrificial giving is not just giving a part of what we own; it is the giving of ourselves, since where our treasure is, there our heart will be also (Matthew 6:21).

When our life and ministry are built with these precious materials, they will endure the fire and please the Lord. These private spiritual disciplines are like those building materials that are found underground. They were subject to tremendous heat and pressure. They are costly, just as prayer, fasting, and giving are costly to us.

It is time to stop offering to the Lord that which costs us nothing. It is not about how great our life looks in the eyes of men; it is the fire of God that will judge our work. If our success isn't built with materials that are fireproof, our work won't last for eternity. We will still be saved, but we will forfeit our reward. That is why it is essential to dedicate ourselves to much prayer, fasting, and giving.

Wood, hay, and straw are discovered on top of the ground, come in large quantities, are cheap, are very common, and can be destroyed by fire. This speaks of a life that is built on pride, carnality, and secret sin

GOLD, SILVER, AND PRECIOUS STONES

instead of a consecrated life built in the secret place. These materials represent living a life of prayerlessness, busyness, and compromise. We are not called to be busy but to be fruitful.

Fruitfulness is only a result of intimacy and abiding in the Holy Spirit. People have become obsessed with becoming popular rather than being pure. It is easy to build with wood, hay, and straw and neglect our private life with God. With proper gifts and skills, we can build big things for God. But Christian life and ministry are different from a business—they flow out of a relationship with God and not from our own efforts. Real ministry is an overflow of the secret place.

As you are fasting, you might find it hard to endure, but take courage; you are building with costly material. As you prioritize prayer and Scripture reading, you are building with rare and precious materials found underground. Don't be discouraged with how big or small things are in your life today. Leave that in God's hands. Your job is to build with excellent materials, and your task is to live a life that you will not be ashamed of on the Day of Judgment.

FAST FORWARD

○ *Prayer*

God, thank You for the promise of eternal life. I am thankful that I have eternal rewards awaiting me. Help my mind to be fixed on the weight of eternity instead of the temporary trials and hardships I face. Develop in me a greater love for Your Word and for intimacy with You.

✶ *Ponder*

What is something that has been on your heart today?

GOLD, SILVER, AND PRECIOUS STONES

Scriptures to meditate on:

1 Then the king said to Araunah, "No, but I will surely buy it from you for a price; nor will I offer burnt offerings to the Lord my God with that which costs me nothing." So David bought the threshing floor and the oxen for fifty shekels of silver.

2 Samuel 24:24

2 For no other foundation can anyone lay than that which is laid, which is Jesus Christ. Now if anyone builds on this foundation with gold, silver, precious stones, wood, hay, straw, each one's work will become clear; for the Day will declare it, because it will be revealed by fire; and the fire will test each one's work, of what sort it is. If anyone's work which he has built on it endures, he will receive a reward. If anyone's work is burned, he will suffer loss; but he himself will be saved, yet so as through fire.

1 Corinthians 3:11–15

FAST FORWARD

I am the true vine, and My Father is the vinedresser. Every branch in Me that does not bear fruit He takes away; and every branch that bears fruit He prunes, that it may bear more fruit. You are already clean because of the word which I have spoken to you. Abide in Me, and I in you. As the branch cannot bear fruit of itself, unless it abides in the vine, neither can you, unless you abide in Me. "I am the vine, you are the branches. He who abides in Me, and I in him, bears much fruit; for without Me you can do nothing. If anyone does not abide in Me, he is cast out as a branch and is withered; and they gather them and throw them into the fire, and they are burned. If you abide in Me, and My words abide in you, you will ask what you desire, and it shall be done for you. By this My Father is glorified, that you bear much fruit; so you will be My disciples."

John 15:1–8

FASTING TIP

Aside from long-term brain health benefits, many people report clearer thinking, faster memory recall, and improved mood while fasting. [4]

DAY EIGHTEEN

VIRAL REVIVAL

> If My people who are called by My name will humble themselves, and pray and seek My face, and turn from their wicked ways, then I will hear from heaven, and will forgive their sin and heal their land.
>
> 2 Chronicles 7:14

In 2018, students organized a march in support of gun control called March for Our Lives. This demonstration was in response to the shooting at the Marjory Stoneman Douglas High School. Over two million people joined that march. Young people took the issue of gun control and turned it into a national protest.

In 2019, during the Global Week for Future, around four million school kids took part in 4,500 strikes across 150 nations to push the climate change agenda. They demanded that political leaders force the fossil fuel industry to transition to renewable energy. It was sparked the previous year by a 17-year-old Swedish climate activist, Greta Thunberg, who would skip school on Fridays to strike for climate change. It

FAST FORWARD

is crazy how all of this was led by kids and got worldwide attention.

Just last year during the COVID-19 pandemic, because of the death of George Floyd, massive demonstrations took place in the United States with over 15 million people participating. It was considered the largest movement in United States history. There were protests, rioting, and looting in countless places. All of this happened while the whole world was shut down—businesses were closed, churches were in lockdown, and social distancing was supposed to be enforced. Large crowds were prohibited, yet this issue was so important to the people of the United States that all the COVID—19 restrictions were ignored. Most governors could say or do nothing about it.

Talk about things going viral! My goal today is not to address social issues, even though they are important and are mentioned in the Bible. God wants revival to be viral. If issues of guns, climate, and police shooting can become viral, how much more should the message of salvation be just as viral?

This has happened before. Revival was "viral" during the First Great Awakening in America when Jonathan Edwards and George Whitefield were preaching. They say that eighty percent of American colonists heard George preach personally, during a time without television or radio. During the Second Great Awakening, one in every fifteen Americans belonged to an evangelical church. The same happened during the Businessman's Revival, the Civil War Revival, the Urban Revivals, and the Azusa Street Revival. The message of the gospel spread like wildfire. It

GOLD, SILVER, AND PRECIOUS STONES

happened again during the Latter Rain Revival and the Healing Revival, the rise of Bill Bright with Campus Crusade for Christ, and the crusades of Billy Graham. Viral revival is nothing new, it has happened before and God wants to do it again. This is more than just touching your family, church, and community—when revival becomes viral, it impacts the nation.

When I use the phrase 'viral revival', I am not referring to some protests, marches, or a few reforms in the Constitution. We have all heard about the impact of the Jesus Movement, the Toronto Blessing, and the Brownsville Revival, which left a lasting impact on the world. God is far more interested in transforming hearts than just reforming a few laws of the land.

God gave us a recipe for widespread viral revival. This recipe is not new. Heaven shutting, rain stopping, drought occurring, locust devouring, and pestilence running rampant are among the many motivations to start seeking God. Maybe there has been a season of spiritual dryness or a demonic attack on your own life and ministry. God has set the pattern that can shift the spiritual atmosphere in your life.

FAST FORWARD

At the beginning of this chapter, you read 2 Chronicles 7:14. Here is the recipe found within:

If My people...	This means that revival doesn't depend on the world, but on His Church.
Humble themselves	As we already discussed, fasting is the biblical way to humility. I encourage you not to wait for God to humble you; obey His instructions and humble yourself. God's people will either humble themselves or be humbled by Him.
Pray	Fasting must lead to fervent praying. Churches must return to being houses of prayer once again.
Seek My face	This means to abandon distractions of this world and pursue the face of God.
Turn from their wicked ways	Fasting, praying, and pursuit will lead to sanctification. Repentance and turning from wicked ways are always the outcome of humility and prayer.

GOLD, SILVER, AND PRECIOUS STONES

Now here is the promise of God:

> *I will hear from heaven and forgive their sins and heal their land*

Heaven will not pour out spiritual rain until the earth pours out prayers of repentance. If the earth doesn't turn to repentance, heaven has no rain to give. God doesn't stop with only forgiveness; He promises to heal our land. God wants to bring revival to our lives, communities, and nations. He desires to make revival viral once again through us. Our goal is to make revival *vital*, but God's job is to make that revival *viral*.

May our fasting lead us to repentance so that God will usher in a revival!

FAST FORWARD

○ *Prayer*

Lord, I want to be a part of what You desire to do here on earth. Purify my heart. I repent of any hidden sin, any arrogance, and wickedness hiding within me. I turn away from anything that displeases You. I ask that You be my greatest desire and that You would once again bring revival to my life, my home, and my nation.

 Ponder

What is an area where you notice the need for revival?

GOLD, SILVER, AND PRECIOUS STONES

Scriptures to meditate on:

1 When I shut up heaven and there is no rain, or command the locusts to devour the land, or send pestilence among My people, if My people who are called by My name will humble themselves, and pray and seek My face, and turn from their wicked ways, then I will hear from heaven, and will forgive their sin and heal their land.

2 Chronicles 7:13–14

2 Will You not revive us again, that Your people may rejoice in You?

Psalm 85:6

3 Create in me a clean heart, O God, and renew a steadfast spirit within me.

Psalm 51:10

4 Repent therefore and be converted, that your sins may be blotted out, so that times of refreshing may come from the presence of the Lord, and that He may send Jesus Christ, who was preached to you before.

Acts 3:19–20

FASTING TIP

Stage four occurs sometime around day 16 and continues through the duration of your fast. While there may be some changes moving beyond this juncture, you will start to feel well balanced. [1]

DAY NINETEEN

BE A FINISHER, NOT A QUITTER

> I have fought the good fight, I have finished the race, I have kept the faith.
>
> 2 Timothy 4:7

A crown belongs to the finisher, not to the starter. So many people begin things and don't finish them—they are great at starting things, but they don't endure to the finish line. You probably know someone who begins diets but quits as soon as they see a cake. They decide to read through the Bible in one year but stop in the book of Leviticus. They start writing a blog, start a YouTube vlog, or begin to write a book, and then they stop. Starting and then quitting halfway can become a habit that will follow you into every area of your life.

The same can happen with your fasting. Many people have the habit of not finishing their fasts. If they decide to fast for 21 days, they stop short at day 19. If they start a three-day fast, they stop on the second day. Now, I do not want to bring guilt to those who stop fasting short of their goal, but what I am after here is to develop the mindset of a "finisher" in you. Develop good habits with fasting and they will spread in every area of your life. Don't quit fasting—finish! Don't be a quitter; be a finisher.

Jesus is called the *finisher* of our faith, not just the author. He is our example to go for total victory and not settle for a partial one. I cannot tell you how many people I have met who started writing a book but never finished it. It is as though it is normal to be the author of something but not a finisher. So a great place to start to develop the habit of finishing what you start is fasting. Go to the end with fasting; don't stop when it's hard. Stop only when you're done. Even on the cross, Jesus exclaimed, it is *finished* when He was finished! For too many people, the words that come out of their mouth are, "It's too hard! I quit!"

There is a story of a king who came to Elisha when the prophet was on his deathbed. Elisha instructed him to get arrows and start striking the ground. The king hit the ground three times and then stopped. It angered the prophet, and he said, *"You should have struck five or six times; then you would have struck Syria till you had completely destroyed it! But now you will strike Syria only three times"* (2 Kings 13:19). I wonder how many people have this same attitude: they try three times and then stop. They stop when they get tired. They stop when they lose interest or motivation. They stop when it gets hard. They quit too early. Therefore, they can't walk in complete victory because they only have a partial commitment.

BE A FINISHER, NOT A QUITTER

○ Prayer

Lord, I thank You for the strength You've given me up till today for this fast. I pray that as I continue, You will break the mindset of limitation off of me. Lord, in any area of my life where I have a hard time ending what I begin, reveal it to me and give me the mental strength to finish. Shift my mindset to be determined and unshakable. Let my words carry weight, that my "yes" will be yes, and my "no" will be no.

✺ Ponder

What is one area you desire to change or grow in? How can you practically accomplish that?

FAST FORWARD

Scriptures to meditate on:

1
Looking unto Jesus, the author and finisher of our faith, who for the joy that was set before Him endured the cross, despising the shame, and has sat down at the right hand of the throne of God.

Hebrews 12:2

2
Blessed is the man who walks not in the counsel of the ungodly, nor stands in the path of sinners, nor sits in the seat of the scornful; but his delight is in the law of the Lord, and in His law he meditates day and night. He shall be like a tree planted by the rivers of water, that brings forth its fruit in its season, whose leaf also shall not wither; and whatever he does shall prosper.

Psalm 1:1–3

3
The fear of the wicked will come upon him, and the desire of the righteous will be granted.

Proverbs 10:24

BE A FINISHER, NOT A QUITTER

4   But let him ask in faith, with no doubting, for he who doubts is like a wave of the sea driven and tossed by the wind. For let not that man suppose that he will receive anything from the Lord; he is a double-minded man, unstable in all his ways.

James 1:6–8

5   Then Jesus said to His disciples, "If anyone desires to come after Me, let him deny himself, and take up his cross, and follow Me."

Matthew 16:24

6   "I am the vine, you are the branches. He who abides in Me, and I in him, bears much fruit; for without Me you can do nothing."

John 15:5

7   I have fought the good fight, I have finished the race, I have kept the faith.

2 Timothy 4:7

FASTING TIP

For those that have made it this far, there shouldn't be any drastic shifts that occur in how you feel physically, and that's okay for this stage of the fast. Instead, a steady balance seems to set in. [1]

DAY TWENTY

SOMEONE IS LIVING IN REVIVAL

> I was alive once without the law, but when the commandment came, sin revived and I died.
>
> Romans 7:9

With one billion monthly active users, Instagram is one of the most popular social networks in the world. Recently, Instagram released an update for its users to be able to follow someone and mute their stories and their posts. In other words, when you follow them, it sends a message that you are really interested in them, but by muting them you are simply not seeing anything they post. I will be the first one to admit my guilt of being overjoyed with this new feature. I muted many people. Sorry about that, but I don't have enough guts to unfollow, and yet I don't have enough time or patience to keep up with them.

One time in prayer, the Holy Spirit highlighted in my mind that so many believers follow the Lord the very same way. Publicly they claim to follow Him, but privately they mute His voice. They profess Jesus but they don't let Jesus possess them, lead them, fill them, or change them. His voice in their life is on "mute." It's not that God isn't speaking; it's that they have decided ahead of time that they will ignore certain things that are "posted." Fasting is too radical. Praying is too boring. Bible reading is just not interesting. Sharing their faith is just too awkward. Serving at the local church is too time consuming. Oh, and giving—they can't afford to do that since they have too many bills and debts to pay. They are "following" Jesus but muting their Friend who intensely loves them.

These people are like wells without water, clouds without rain, lukewarm, neither hot nor cold. They are living on the fence. They have enough of the world that they aren't fully living for God, yet they have enough of God that they can't fully enjoy the world. What an empty way to live Christianity!

Paul wrote in a letter to the Romans: *"sin revived and I died."* Of course, Paul was talking about the strict commandments of God and that they have no power to produce life and holiness. Sin revived, along with self and guilt. In Paul's life, sin experienced revival, and that revival brought him death.

What if I were to point out to you that someone could be living in a revival, but that revival might be his sinful self, not his spirit? Could it be entertainment is in revival in your life and not your prayer life? Could it be lust that has revived and not your purity? It could be laziness that has a breakthrough instead of discipline. Someone is having a revival, but what has been revived? What gets you excited?

SOMEONE IS LIVING IN REVIVAL

When sin revives, you die. When your spirit has revival, sin dies.

Spiritual revival is the best protection against living in sin. The best way to end the struggle with sin is to choose a life of surrender to the Holy Spirit. The passion with which you served the devil you will now use to serve God. Some call that radical, but I see it as a replacement. If you used to spend your time, your money, and your life on things that only leave you empty and unfulfilled, how much more should you go all the way for the Lord? You will never know what God has prepared for you until you go all the way. So many people are disappointed with Jesus because they are expecting His full-time benefits, but they are living as part-time believers. Don't fear what it will cost you; Jesus is worthy of everything you are afraid of losing.

Paul started the verse with "I was alive once." Maybe that describes you. You used to burn for Jesus. You were once on fire. You had great passion for the Lord. But what happened? Certain desires, passions, or self-interests came. Maybe in your case, it was a girlfriend that came into your life, or college, or a career, or a family. Sometimes it's the good things that distract us from God's best. It can even be a ministry that distracts us from Jesus. As with Martha, serving others can bring a lot of unnecessary worry and busyness.

My goal is not to guilt trip you, but to awaken your love for Jesus. I want to spark a new passion for His presence in you so that you really really want to pursue His purpose for your life. My prayer for you is that

FAST FORWARD

you cannot remember a time when you loved Jesus more than you do today. Today is the day of revival for your spirit, for your prayer life, and for your consecration. It is time to ruin sin's revival and get the Holy Spirit revival. Jump off the fence and join the pursuit of the Holy One. Unmute the voice and listen to the conviction of the Holy Spirit; don't settle for speaking in tongues. Get unstuck today by making revival a lifestyle, not an occasional event. Come out of the rut of your flesh and into revival in your spirit!

SOMEONE IS LIVING IN REVIVAL

○ Prayer

God, I don't want anything in my life to revive that isn't of You. Revive a new love for You within me; revive a passion for Your Word; awaken a love for the lost within me. And kill all that tries to distract me from following You with all my heart.

Ponder

What does a revived spiritual life look like to you? What are some ways you can begin or continue to revive that fire?

FAST FORWARD

Scriptures to meditate on:

1. I was alive once without the law, but when the commandment came, sin revived and I died.

Romans 7:9

2. And Elijah came to all the people, and said, "How long will you falter between two opinions? If the LORD is God, follow Him; but if Baal, follow him." But the people answered him not a word.

1 Kings 18:21

3. These are wells without water, clouds carried by a tempest, for whom is reserved the blackness of darkness forever.

2 Peter 2:17

4. Nevertheless I have this against you, that you have left your first love.

Revelation 2:4

SOMEONE IS LIVING IN REVIVAL

Adulterers and adulteresses! Do you not know that friendship with the world is enmity with God? Whoever therefore wants to be a friend of the world makes himself an enemy of God. Or do you think that the Scripture says in vain, "The Spirit who dwells in us yearns jealously"?

James 4:4–5

"Now therefore, fear the Lord, serve Him in sincerity and in truth, and put away the gods which your fathers served on the other side of the River and in Egypt. Serve the Lord! And if it seems evil to you to serve the Lord, choose for yourselves this day whom you will serve, whether the gods which your fathers served that were on the other side of the River, or the gods of the Amorites, in whose land you dwell. But as for me and my house, we will serve the Lord."

Joshua 24:14–15

FASTING TIP

How you choose to end your fast is critical. Depending on how long you fast, you may need to ease your way back into eating solid food. Fruit juices, cooked vegetables, and broths can help acclimate your body and digestive system to eating as internal mechanisms come back online. [1]

DAY TWENTY-ONE

FROM GRAPES TO GLORY

> His mother said to the servants, "Whatever He says to you, do it."
>
> Romans 7:9

During the 40-day fast, the Holy Spirit taught me something from the first miracle that Jesus performed and I want to share it with you.

Jesus turned water into wine, which is totally miraculous and impossible. Water, unlike grapes, doesn't have what it takes to become wine. Grapes transform into wine with time and through a certain process, but water turns to wine only by a miracle. There was one primary key to that miracle—obedience. When the servants obeyed Jesus, God turned the water into wine.

If you are willing to be a servant and obey Jesus, God will do the same in your life. You might not have the right education to be successful. You might not have the right connections to make it in life. You might have been born on the wrong side of the tracks or have been dealt a bad hand in life. Time might be an issue for you. The question is not if you have what it takes; the real question is: Are you willing to do what He says? When you don't have what it takes, do whatever He says. You will see God take your weakness and turn it into strength; He will take water and make it wine.

Obedience in the area of finances releases God's miracles. Doing what God says in the area of ministry puts His blessing on it. When you don't have what it takes to be successful, focus on doing what it takes to be an obedient servant to the Holy Spirit. At times, obeying the Holy Spirit may seem ridiculous, but that is the key to radical miracles. What the servants did was crazy—but it was crazy only until the miracle happened!

Even though grapes have what it takes to be wine, but they can't become wine unless they are willing to go through crushing. Oh, how we hate crushing! There are people who are gifted, skilled, and connected; I call them grapes. God wants to turn grapes into wine. He wants to take you further and release His anointing in your life. That happens through crushing.

Another miracle Jesus performed is when He faced a crowd of hungry people, He took the bread that was given to Him and blessed it. After blessing it, He broke it. Only then did it become a blessing to the multitude and much was left over. Whatever God breaks, He turns it into a blessing.

God wants to take you from being blessed to being a blessing to others, and this comes through the process of breaking and crushing. Breaking your pride, ego, selfishness, and sinful tendencies will pave the way to make you a blessing to the world. You can remain the way you are: gifted to some degree with a certain level of influence and grace on your life, or you can go further by allowing the Holy Spirit to take you to a place of being humble and contrite in spirit (Isaiah 66:2). I am not talking about abuse or self-inflicted suffering. Take Joshua, for example. He knew that the only way for the children of Israel to see a new level of God's miracles tomorrow was to start sanctifying themselves today: *"And Joshua said to the people, 'Sanctify yourselves, for tomorrow the Lord will do wonders among you'"* (Joshua 3:5). Today's sanctification brings tomorrow's success. Today's fasting brings tomorrow's favor. Today's prayers bring tomorrow's power.

Are you like water that God is wanting to turn into wine? Or are you like grapes that God is wanting to turn into wine? Either way, obedience and consecration are the way to new levels in the Holy Spirit. If you, as a grape, reach a certain level with God but refuse to continue to grow in your sanctification, you will dry up. Grapes become raisins with time. They lose their juice. Time by itself doesn't turn grapes into wine; crushing does that. Time turns grapes into raisins. If you don't sanctify your life, time will turn you into a raisin, not wine. Time doesn't turn talents into glory. If you are God's chosen grape but you refuse crushing, you will end up as a dried-out raisin. Choose the way of the cross. Embrace the suffering that follows obedience to the Holy Spirit.

FAST FORWARD

Remember: Jesus is worthy of everything you are afraid of losing. Don't pray to become a bigger and better grape; surrender to become wine! If you lost your juice, if you stop surrendering, if your gifts become your idol – go back there and repent. Rehydrate by immersing yourself in the rivers of Living Water.

Prayer

Father, I thank You for what You are doing in me through this fast. I give you permission to break all pride and stubbornness within me; break off any fear that hinders me from fully obeying You. I surrender my will to You. I desire to obey You even in the small things. Give me the grace to follow You. Bring to my remembrance the words You last spoke to me, and give me the courage to obey, no matter the cost.

Ponder

What has been the hardest part about this fast? What has been the most rewarding part?

FAST FORWARD

Scriptures to meditate on:

1
And Joshua said to the people, "Sanctify yourselves, for tomorrow the Lord will do wonders among you."

Joshua 3:5

2
But in a great house there are not only vessels of gold and silver, but also of wood and clay, some for honor and some for dishonor. Therefore if anyone cleanses himself from the latter, he will be a vessel for honor, sanctified and useful for the Master, prepared for every good work. Flee also youthful lusts; but pursue righteousness, faith, love, peace with those who call on the Lord out of a pure heart.

2 Timothy 2:20–22

3
Most assuredly, I say to you, unless a grain of wheat falls into the ground and dies, it remains alone; but if it dies, it produces much grain.

John 12:24

4 Then He took the five loaves and the two fish, and looking up to heaven, He blessed and broke them, and gave them to the disciples to set before the multitude.

Luke 9:16

5 Thus says the Lord: "Heaven is My throne, and earth is My footstool. Where is the house that you will build Me? And where is the place of My rest? For all those things My hand has made, and all those things exist," says the Lord. "But on this one will I look: On him who is poor and of a contrite spirit, and who trembles at My word."

Isaiah 66:1-2

FASTING TIP

Stage four is the extension and completion of the healing and cleansing processes that began during the earlier stages. The longer you fast, the more time and opportunity your body has to heal and cleanse itself. [1]

APPENDIX ONE

ABOUT THE AUTHOR

Vladimir Savchuk is a rising spiritual voice that God is using to profoundly impact this generation. Leveraging modern media technology to propagate the timeless truth of the faith, Pastor Vlad has written books, hosted conferences, and created content platforms that are touching thousands of people all around the world.

Pastor Vlad's creative approach in leading Hungry Generation church has been used by the Holy Spirit to cultivate an anointed internship program and a worship culture with worldwide reach. He is a gifted speaker with an emphasis on rarely-addressed spiritual topics such as spiritual warfare, deliverance and the Holy Spirit. Pastor Vlad is declaring ancient truths in a modern way.

He is married to his beautiful wife, Lana, with whom he enjoys spending time and doing ministry together.

APPENDIX TWO

OTHER BOOKS

Break Free
How to Get Free and Stay Free

Single, Ready to Mingle
God's Principles for Relating, Dating, and Mating

Fight Back
Moving from Deliverance to Dominion

Available everywhere books are sold in paperback, electronic, and audio version. You can also download a free PDF on www.pastorvlad.org/books

APPENDIX THREE

ONLINE COURSES

In 2020, Pastor Vlad launched online courses to impact the world by training up the laborers for God's harvest field. Many believers around the world don't have the time to go to Bible school or can't afford Bible training. Therefore, we make our online school completely free.

VladSchool consists of courses that are Spirit-filled, practical, and scriptural about powerful topics such as deliverance, the Holy Spirit, prayer, ministry, identity in Christ, etc. All of our classes are offered for free, thanks to the generous support of our partners.

Enroll today at www.vladschool.com to grow in the Lord and to be trained in ministry.

APPENDIX FOUR

STAY CONNECTED

facebook.com/vladhungrygen

twitter.com/vladhungrygen

instagram.com/vladhungrygen

youtube.com/vladimirsavchuk

www.pastorvlad.org

www.vladschool.com

If you have a testimony from reading this book, please email *hello@pastorvlad.org*

If you wish to post about this book on your social media, please use tag *@vladhungrygen* and use the *#pastorvlad* hashtag.

APPENDIX FIVE

REFERENCES

1. Global Healing
   2021
   "The Stages of Fasting: What Happens To Your Body When You Fast?"
   Global Healing
   https://explore.globalhealing.com/stages-of-fasting-what-happens-when-you-fast

2. The Health Guide
   2018
   "12 Thrilling Benefits of Fasting."
   Wikipedia
   https://besthealth.guide/12-thrilling-benefits-of-fasting

3. Brennan, Dan
   2021
   "How Fasting Can Benefit Your Mental Health"
   WebMD
   https://www.webmd.com/diet/psychological-benefits-of-fasting

4. Mattson MP
   2005
   "Energy Intake, Meal Frequency, And Health: A Neurobiological Perspective"
   6. 10.1146/annurev.nutr.25.050304.092526

APPENDIX SIX

CREDITS

Editing: Everett Roeth, Lubov Kasyanov
Cover design: Nazar Parkhotyuk
Interior design: Max Banmann

Made in the USA
Las Vegas, NV
07 January 2024

84058404R00105